TRUMPSTERS & TRAITORS 2:

Trump or America: Your Choice

By Richard Neil Graham
San Diego, California, USA

Published by LA NY Edit

LA·NY
Edit

I0101117

Graham, Richard Neil,
1958 –
Trumpsters & Traitors 2

Printed in USA by Kindle Direct Publishing
ISBN-13: 978-0-9834060-7-5
ISBN-10: 0983406073

Library of Congress Control Number: Unable to acquire due to Trump Covid Clusterf-ck.

LA NY Edit, San Diego, California, USA

Cover Art: Mohammed Lincoln Washington, Esquire IV

Cover Design: TBW

Table of Contents

Acknowledgments

Many thanks to Mohammed Jefferson Lincoln IV for the cover artwork, to TBW for the cover design, and to Scot Gassen for his foreword. Thanks to Jeff Cooper for the last-minute editing suggestions. Thanks to everyone in Nasty Women & Bad Hombres (you know who you are) for your friendship and support during the writing of this book.

Donald Trump himself, of course, must be thanked. He gave me something to do that could keep my busy butt out of jail, at least until his potential second term. Then, as we all know, all bets would be off.

The Republican party as a whole, because they've proved that there is not one single Republican politician with enough political courage to stand up to Donald Trump. Traitors at worst, wimps at best.

Everyone in the Trump administration, current or past. All have proved to be cowardly, ridiculous, embarrassing and traitorous by turns. May you all get your just desserts.

All other contributors have asked to remain anonymous. I can't understand why.

Author's Note

This is a schizophrenic book. The last four years have been a tragedy of the absurd and horrifying. Yet I still pray for a blue tsunami and hope for a miracle. Ain't that schizophrenic? Millions of Americans have gone from guarded optimism to utter horror, with every major court decision something to cheer or despair. (Usually despair.)

Congress has given us up to Russia, and you know all about the "executive" branch's thousands of documented lies. I hope this is my last Trump joke book and that he'll be defeated a few days from now. If he "wins," I'll be forced to write more of these books, because I've made it my life's goal to witness and document Trump's eventual defeat and disappearance from American public life. If he's "reelected," I'll gnash my teeth for a week or a month and then get back to writing these sad diatribes against the worst leader America has ever had the misfortune to witness... and to suffer.

When it all ends in an ugly crash for Donald Trump and his family of grifters, the damage they've caused will never fully be repaired. You can't bring back dead seekers of refuge or give back stolen careers, and dead landscapes take a mighty long time to heal. The majority of Americans agree, and that blame will be spread across both American political parties - the party in power for crimes of commission, the other for crimes of omission - not fighting hard enough against Trump.

Even after Trump "won" in 2016, he continued to pander to his fanatical base, loudly megaphoning conspiracy theories and other ridiculous baloney. Trump was planting conspiracy theories even before the 2016 election, so, that if he lost, it would be because it was "rigged" in Hillary's favor.

We're losing the fresh water, clean skies and national parks that we've accepted as our birthright as Americans. I'll gladly continue to fight against Trumpism for clean water, for clear skies and for protected national parks, because I know that their value is without measure. They need to be defended against a man in a golden tower whose idea of nature is the cooling breeze of Fatboy Defining Finishing Flexible Hairspray in an 8 ounce bottle. (You could look it up.)

You've a right and an obligation to vote. Hundreds of thousands of people have literally given their lives to give you the opportunity. So, drag yourself to a mailbox with ballot in hand, deposit it, and put one more nail in the coffin of a presidency that never should have survived a trip down that stupid escalator.

I love America and want its dream to survive. Let's kick out Trump on November 3 and place our worst modern mistake in America's rear-view mirror.

Richard Neil Graham
San Diego, California
November 3, 2020

Foreword

Not even the infamous New York grifter who staged a laughable attention-seeking publicity stunt by riding the escalator down in Trump Tower with trophy wife Melania in tow circa 2015 to announce his intentions to launch a presidential candidacy believed he would be slimed into the White House after "winning" the 2016 presidential election.

It's now nearly five years later, with multiple indefensible scandals, gaffes galore, impeachment in the House of Representatives over powerful evidence of self-dealing through traitorous collusion with Russia, a hostile foreign power. Add grotesque incompetence (including the negligent criminal mismanagement of a catastrophic pandemic with thousands of fatalities and a debilitating economic downturn), the stumblebum masquerading in the guise of POTUS still has a cult following populated by millions of red-MAGA-dunce-cap-wearing supporters.

The dynamic that keeps the majority of his base still riveted into place can be explained by the fear-driven, white-supremacist movement that was awakened during President Obama's two terms as America's first black president. Trump used hate speech to ignite and harness that far-right reactionary energy to forge a coalition within the GOP for a narrow win by a margin of 70,000 votes in the antiquated Electoral College. This unfairly eclipsed Hillary Clinton's vast advantage of nearly three *million* popular votes.

So here we are today on the cusp of the 2020 presidential election with the most incompetent, corrupt, traitorous president in U.S. history, with a base of willfully ignorant supporters unpersuadable by facts and reason and who comprise roughly 40 percent of the electorate. Those loyalists will stick with Trump regardless of his lack in decorum and levels of criminality as long as he triggers the libs and "owns the Dems" while insisting they're the flag-wavin', Bible-thumpin', white-picket-fence-lovin', *real* Americans.

Meanwhile, with a continuous stream of easily debunked lies and preposterous reality-TV-styled outrages coming from the poseur in the Oval Office, the U.S. has lost trust and credibility by being considered a laughingstock and feared as a destabilizing loose cannon within the world community. Der Trumpenhoaxer's irrational behavior and the unwavering support from the sell-out Retrumplican Congressional stooges with their cheering throngs of MAGAs create a political theater of the absurd, which make this bizarre unreality seem as hallucinatory as Salvador Dali's surrealist painting of a dreamscape replete with melting time pieces.

So, the serious condition of a nation gone horribly wrong from the slapstick comedy of errors delivered by a prodigious cast of bad actors validate the zingers of truth proffered by Richard Neil Graham within his edgy political satire as especially timely and cogent.

Scott Gassen
Columbus, Ohio

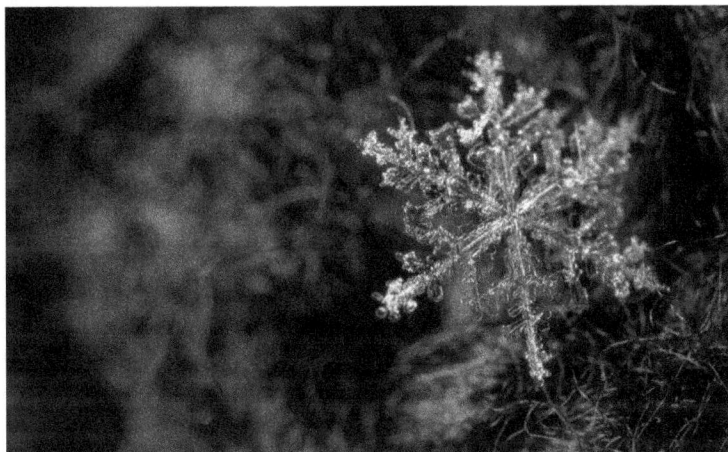

SUCH SNOWFLAKES THESE TRUMPSTERS BE!

True story. I'm at Patrick's Bar in downtown San Diego on September 25, 2019. I figured that I'd listen to some blues by a band with Johnny V., a guitarist whom I would soon learn had played on Elvin Bishop's "Fooled Around and Fell in Love," way back when.

After the show, a long-haired dude at the bar challenged me to a music trivia competition. While I'm trying to figure out my question, I show him and friend a copy of Trumpsters & Traitors, my new joke book.

The long-haired dude passes it back to me without comment. I don't notice this until later. I hand my book back to his friend who flips through it and smiles. I come up with a trivia question and tell the long-haired dude that I have a question for him, touching him on the shoulder to get his attention.

He screams, "He touched me!" as if I had inserted a cattle prod up his ample ass.

Dumbfounded, I try to ask him what's wrong, when the lady bartender gets in my face and says, "Get out!"

I said, "I didn't *do* anything!"

She said, "I *know* him. I don't know you."

I feel a presence behind me, and it's the bouncer.

"You have to go," he says.

I say, "I haven't had a chance to drink my beer."

Bartender says, "I won't charge you for it, but you've got to pay for your first."

I paid it, left a big fat "0" for a tip, and walked out.

I quickly realized what had happened. It wasn't that I touched the long-haired dude on the shoulder. It was that I showed him Trumpsters & Traitors.

Such snowflakes these Trumpsters be!

PALE GARBAGE

I never dreamed I'd trash an American president. But then, I never could have imagined Twitter or "President" Trump.

When a North Korean dictator tells you who your president is, believe him the first time. Trump is definitely a dotard.

Vladimir Putin lost a long time ago. Donald Trump gave him new life.

Triggered by treason? You're damn straight I am. Why aren't you?

"Trump" means never saying you're sorry. It also means to cut a fart.

If we survive Trump, let's hope that aliens finally show themselves and congratulate us for overcoming the universe's greatest enemy: Trumpism.

Trump promises never to touch your health care, and you should believe him. Once you're dying and need a hand, he won't lift a finger.

Trump won't physically touch your savings, either, but he'll make damn well sure that ever last nickel eventually trickles up to him.

Trump will reveal his new health care plan after the 2020 election. If he wins, he'll push it back to 2024. If he loses (praise god), it won't matter that he's been lying to moronic voters since 2016.

LIAR

On November 4, I voted for Donald Trump! (To go to prison.)

Donald Trump is the guy who promises to pick you up from school, and he does, but not before he sets your books, teachers, transcripts, janitors and school on fire.

Trump will steal the social security benefits that you paid for during your entire life, but he'll justify it in one way or another. He'll say, "Having to work till you're 80 will build your character." Or, "Yes, you paid into it, but unfortunately, with currency that has long been out of circulation." Whatever his story will be, you'll accept it. Why? Because you're stupid, or, like too many of us, you waited too long to fight back.

Trump'$ fir$t prioritie$ are alway$ clear to $ee.

I told an acquaintance that I'd written an anti-Trump joke book, but that I was concerned that he might not like it. He said, "I'm not stupid."

I can't wait until Trump is finally gone and we can argue about sports again.

Trump says he's "The Chosen One." The guillotine answers, "Yes!"

I was taught not to hate. Trump has overcome a lifetime of training.

The only reason that Trump wanted to buy Greenland is that he thought "Greenland" meant Money Land.

I just want Trump out. At least Satan doesn't Tweet.

The best invention in my lifetime is the word processor. Why? Because I'm a lousy typist. With the old Smith Corona typewriter in college, I used up Liquid Paper more often than Trump attorneys use black ink for redactions.

I have tried to keep up with Trump's insanity, but for once, I'm not a sprinter... I'm a marathoner, and I expect to give my testimony when it counts.

America won't achieve moral standing until integrity matters.

Lying like a rug is great in carpeting. Not so much in presidents.

The Emperor has no brains.

Donald Trump can't have any fun at international summits if Putin's not there because his "nyet profits" shrink.

What's the definition of condescending? That's what happens when Donald Trump goes to hell.

I know that there are certain things that you just can't say. But when the president gets away with it every single day, you begin to lose your concept of how low is too low to go.

I'd heard of a Category 5 hurricane before, but that's the last thing I'd concern myself with regarding Trump's lack of knowledge. Nuking one? That's another story altogether.

People that have promoted eugenics include Adolf Hitler, Donald Trump and Jeffrey Epstein. Now there's a Trio of Turds that you really want to listen to!

Trump has no boundaries. He must be stopped. It's up to us.

Tearing kids away from their families is Hitler-like behavior, and Trump owns it.

"The meeting of two dictators," a slip up by a lady Fox News lie-caster describing Trump and Kim Jong-Un, never gets old.

The good thing about having a fanatic as president is that you can say crazy shit, too, at least until you're in the concentration camp.

Donald Trump needs to go back to the shithole he came from. Mar-A-Lago.

I think that Donald Trump is the loneliest man in the world. I'd feel sorry for him if he wasn't concentrated evil.

Trump is an Old Testament profit.

Donald Trump is Mr. Potter from "It's A Wonderful Life" on Adderall.

I know how to spell Donald Trump's favorite thing: $$$$$$.

Trump desperately wants to be loved and respected, but he doesn't know that love and respect are earned, not enforced... and he never will.

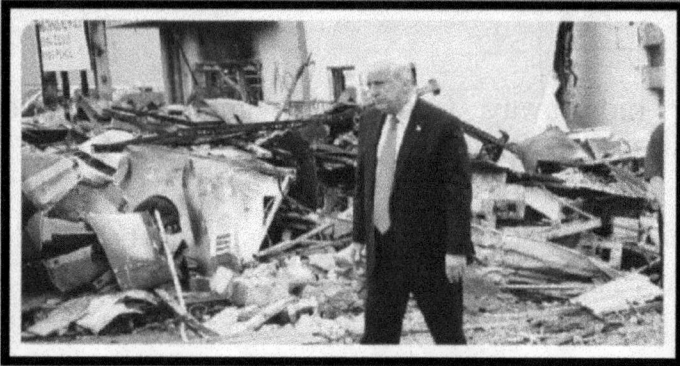

AMERICAN CARNAGE

BROUGHT TO YOU BY DONALD J. TRUMP

Thinking about what Trump's done right? That's almost impossible. It would be like finding a needle in a haystack without even knowing what state the haystack is in.

Trump calls George Conway Moonface, seemingly unaware that Orangeface is not attractive, either.

Trump doesn't care about his wall. He just likes to fuck with brown people.

Trump fucked up badly on this pandemic. If I can't convince you, that's OK. Every town needs its village idiot. You're it.

Trump is obviously dumb, but when it comes to survival, he's like a cockroach that no Republican senator will step on.

Hey Trump, I know a porn star who wants your dick pics. She's Stormy like a hurricane and her cell-phone number is 1-800-CALL-FBI.

Donald Trump thinks that he's a #Sharpie, but he's a #dotard.

I don't want Trump's money or his debts. I don't want his Trump Towers. I don't want his racism. I don't want his xenophobia. I don't want his misogyny. I just want him to go away.

Trump = Fart in Britain, Shit in America.

Trump is working hard to destroy America. But why? The obvious answer is that Putin has Trump by Trump's bb-sized balls.

Trump? He's as dumb as he looks.

You see Trump drowning. What are you throwing him? Me? I'm throwing Covfefe.

I've finally figured it out! Trump is Saudi American!

Donald Trump dresses up in Orangeface and tangerines are *pissed*.

Yes, Trump should be impeached for trading military aid for dirt on a political opponent. But he should have been fired a long time ago for his assault on common decency.

I'd rather my books not sell and Trump disappear than my books sell millions and Trump stay.

Back in the day, we could argue and get mad, but violence wasn't usually the response to a political argument. I blame Trump.

Do me a favor, Trump. Resign.

Trump is pale garbage.

When you Adderall up, I think Trump's on drugs.

If Trump worked as hard as he golfs and tweets, America would be in even worse shape.

Maybe Trump lets people listen in on his bribery and collusion phone calls because he doesn't want to be in prison all alone.

"Integrity" and "Trump" go together like ice cream and cigarette butts.

Fake hair. Tie too long. Dick too short. Brain too small. Mouth too big. Extra-large rump. Whaddya get? T.R.U.M.P. TRUMP!

Trump is the tallest man with a Napoleonic Complex in world history.

Trump thinks that he's America's king, when he's actually Putin's court jester.

Trump demands this. Trump demands that. Pretty soon Trump will be in prison, with predatory goat herders, eating hamberders, and still fat.

Quit waiting for it. There is no low that is too low for Donald Trump.

There are levels of evil. Trump is raising the bar.

I'm Trump-fueled and trigger-fingered these days. It will take some time to get myself back to a somewhat reasonable level of humanity once he's finally gone.

In 2017, the Trump administration demanded information from Facebook on anti-Trump activists. I've been right here all along, #TraitorTrump, you orange byotch.

Trump has betrayed the rule of law, the Constitution, citizens (Otto Warmbier), journalists (Jamal Khashoggi), American soldiers and now the Kurds. He's burning down America institution by institution, yet Republicans in power are mostly silent. What an incredible work of fiction this could have been!

Trump betraying our allies? I did Nazi that coming.

That pee pee tape that Putin is holding over Trump's head must be a doozy.

A buddy says Trump will eventually resign. I say Trump knows that prison awaits, so he fights to his bitter end.

Trump is a Russian ass set.

I respect the office of the President, not the whack job currently trespassing in the Oval Office.

The president of the USA is the most powerful person in the world. Insanity currently rules the world.

What's Trump's best leadership quality? He'll lead you to Hell! (But not back.)

Impeach then deport. Why pay good money on incarcerating Trump? Let Russia enjoy him for the rest of his miserable life.

Trump is a master at protecting himself from future crimes by diminishing their seriousness in advance - for instance, saying he could shoot someone on 5th Avenue in New York City and not lose a voter. So, I'm going on record to say that when I *do* break into Fort Knox and steal as much gold as possible, I won't lose any days of freedom to prison. If I am arrested, I'll just use the Trump Defense. It's working for him... so far.

It's easy to know whether Trump has written a tweet or dictated it. If it has spelling and grammatical errors, it's him. If not, it was dictated.

Nancy Pelosi's got big balls, Trump's got no balls at all!

People say that Donald Trump slurs his words. Donald Trump *is* a slur.

It's fun to mock Trump for his spelling, his lack of intelligence and his embarrassing tweets, but I think that we should concentrate on how his moronity kills.

Someone could shoot someone on 5th Avenue and not give a shit, too, if they hit Trump.

Donald Trump is imploring Republicans to attack the impeachment allegations rather than the process, saying "Go with substance!" Unfortunately, the substance is Adderall.

Trump is the Bi-Polar President. He brings stupid people up and intelligent people down.

America has the most cases of Coronavirus on the planet because our president is the dumbest man on the planet.

Donald Trump has more Teflon than the manufacturer of Teflon.

Donald Trump is as classy as flip flops at a funeral.

Donald Trump is as trustworthy as Hannibal Lecter at a body-building competition.

Dr. Anthony Fauci? Courage often comes in small packages.

Ebola virus was first discovered in 1976 near the Ebola River in what is now the Democratic Republic of Congo. I'm surprised that Trump calls it Ebola and not Congo Disease.

BE BEST

Donald Trump is as worthwhile as a mustache on a mailbox.

Donald Trump is the Chloroqueen.

Donald Trump projects... just like vomit.

Donald Trump's brain is a Republican hoax.

Don't listen to Trump's Coronavirus political rallies. Wait a couple of hours and watch the comedian truth tellers.

American exceptionalism has been a contradiction in terms since about the time of the Berlin Airlift.

Anthony Fauci knows the dangers we face. You know it and I know it. Trump refuses to acknowledge it. Not because he hopes that people won't die. Oh, no. It's much more basic. Trump doesn't want any bad news that might kill his hopes of being reelected and thus avoiding prison or worse.

Be wealthy. Get tested immediately. Be poor. Good luck, chump!

I pissed off a few hockey buddies by supporting Barack Obama back in 2008. They've been getting their revenge ever since Trump came down that fucking escalator.

I saw a woman wearing a crocheted face mask today. It had holes in it the size of peas. I'm guessing it's an Ivanka Trump design.

Before he died, my father told me that corporations once had integrity. When he retired, he nearly lost his pension. Fortunately, he had enough vacation days accrued to get him to his well-deserved pension. Everything had changed, he told me. Money had become premier. Integrity became as valued as the word of a used-car salesman. Two years later, Trump was installed. Both of my parents were gone before Trump came down that escalator preaching hate. Thank you, universe.

Civil liberties don't give you the right to yell *fire!* in a crowded theater, or the right to party with 100 people during a pandemic that your country leads in cases and deaths. Civil liberties *do* give you the right to be a douchebag, and you're doing *bigly* with that.

Come on, Twilight Zone 2020. Please admit that the last four years have only been a preview of a TV-show remake so we can get on with our lives!

I just saw a piece of toilet paper with a Trump clinging to it!

Trump is America's greatest cheater. Either Trump is defeated in 2020, or America is done, and Putin won.

Trump says that he's lost $2 to $5 billion since he became president. Know how I know that's bullshit? He would have resigned a long time ago.

Quid pro quo! Trump has got to go!

Since 2016, America has slipped in U.S. News & World Report's rankings of the the "Best Countries to Live In" from 4th to 8th. Yay, Trump!

Trump will fire those who supported him, one by one, until his last sycophant is gone.

Stephanie Winston Wolkoff, who worked as a contractor for President Donald Trump's 2016 inauguration and an adviser for First Lady Melania Trump, was thrown under the bus. Priebus, Tillerson, Kelly and were thrown under the bus. He threw Colonel Vindman, Fiona Hill, Gordon Sondland, William Taylor and George Kent under the bus. He *will* throw Mike Pompeo, Mick Mulvaney and Don Jr. under the bus, too. Ivanka is safe, only because he wants to date her. America suddenly has a curious shortage of buses.

Just wait, Trumpy. Your time in the barrel is coming.

Recently, Trump had an unscheduled medical exam. No news yet on whether or not he got a moob job.

Trump complains that impeachment has been very tough on his family. WTF? I was 28 when he came into office, and now I'm 62!

Give Clinton head, ruin your life. Give Trump a blowjob, get a job.

Compared to now, my life was perfect before Trump.

Congressional Democrats' biggest mistake is looking at both sides of an issue, as if they were in a high school debate club and not in the highest echelon of power.

Continue to self isolate or trust Trump? Tough decision.

Did you hear about the players on Trump's ice hockey team? They drowned in spring training.

Forgive my typographical errors. Unlike Trump, I have big hands!

If Donald Trump decides to leave the USA after losing to Biden, I understand that Jeffrey Epstein's pedophile island is available.

Truth > Lies.
Truth > Trump.
America > Trump.
Therefore, truth and America > Trump's Lies.

YOUR FACE WHEN YOUR ASS
IS 2 BIG 4 YOUR CHAIR

Herbert Hoover is looking mighty presidential right now.

Here's why Donald Trump can't watch an entire security briefing: to Trump, 15 minutes = 30 Stormy Daniels.

How do I write Trump so well? I think of a president, and I take away reason and accountability.

The Trump Administration is the world's longest Twilight Zone episode.

"Tronald Dump." Bathroom graffiti at Acorn Casino in Campo, California.

I could be a millionaire if I supported Trump, but I prefer to sleep peacefully at night.

Donald Trump said that Nancy Pelosi's teeth are falling out. He should know; his brain fell out years ago.

Nails on a chalkboard, chairs scraped across a floor, screaming children. All are more enjoyable than a Donald Trump speech.

Trump will soon be on the cover of a new magazine! Incarcerated Today.

Trump equates money with intelligence. That's why he surrounds himself with other wealthy morons.

I gotta wonder if Trump would have tried to destroy everything that John McCain did had McCain been president before him and not Obama.

Donald Trump is Gordon Gekko, but without the looks, hair, or intelligence of actor Michael Douglas.

Trump accusing anyone of anything is like Tonya Harding accusing Nancy Kerrigan of stealing her metal rod.

I'm a satirist. I share stupid stuff like images of Donald Trump wearing a turban. I'm not the president. If I were, I'd hope that I had more important things to do than post images of Nancy Pelosi and Chuck Schumer wearing turbans.

Donald Trump supporters say that he makes "libtards" like me cry. I don't cry much, but I am quite devastated about how quickly a country can turn to fascism.

Donald Trump's gonna live past 100. Why? All of the preservatives in Big Macs and fries.

Donald Trump is the male Roseanne Roseannadanna; just not as self aware… or funny.

Get that sonofabitch out of the White House!

The Mayhem character in the Allstate insurance ads? That's Trump.

Trump's autobiography should have been called "The Art of the Steal." When has Trump ever made a successful deal, besides secret ones with Vladimir Putin?

How do I know that Trump didn't write The Art of the Deal? Because it's not full of misspellings and odd capitalization, and I *know* that he didn't know what "hyperbole" means. And considering Trump's propensity for grabbing women by the pussy, it could have been called "The Art of the Feel," though that's much too kind. "The Creep of Queens" would be more accurate.

What's with the canard that Trump wrote books, anyway? Books and Trump go together like Trump and the Constitution, or Trump and integrity, or Trump and empathy. They don't.

I write books. To write books, you must have first *read* books. Trump doesn't read books. Hell, he doesn't even read important military briefings if they don't have cartoons and 40-point fonts.

I was disappointed when interest on savings accounts went from 5 and 6 percent to almost nothing under Reagan. I was upset when H.W. Bush started a war based on lies about Iraq's weapons of mass destruction. But I'm gobsmacked by how much destruction that Donald Trump has caused in his first term. I'd exhume Reagan and unretire GWB if only it meant that it would be the last time I'd ever have to hear the expletive "Trump."

Twitter and Facebook enable fascism. Theodore Roosevelt knew how to handle monopolies. Unfortunately, we currently have a president who couldn't carry TR's jock strap. That he benefits from those companies' monopolies is just an ugly side issue.

I missed a space while typing and then realized that it wasn't really a typo: "Trump: This moment inhuman history."

Trump accusing anyone of *anything* is like Cheech Marin accusing Tommy Chong of inhaling.

Women often do not understand it when men talk "smack" - insulting each other. It's actually a way of expressing love... *and* keeping your friends from getting too high and mighty. Trump never got any of that leveling banter because he has no friends. That's why he's such a dick.

Trump: Stupid is as hateful does.

Trump is the high school bully that karma hasn't caught up with yet.

Donald, you ain't the sharpest tool in the shed... but you're still a tool.

Donald Trump's Native American name: Runs from Water.

Trump's major hair problem is that he can't read: He buys Hair Die.

If Trump promotes it, it's *bunk*.

Imagine, an unhinged president in the time of a global pandemic. What a thrilling fictional novel it could be!

Like sharks need to keep moving to stay alive, Donald Trump needs to keep lying to stay in power.

Looking at Donald Trump and seeing a savior is like looking at Ronald McDonald and seeing a nutritionist.

How many Donald Trumps does it take to ruin a country? Just one.

BEN CARSON PERFORMED

MY LOBOTOMY

I admit it. I have Trump Derangement Syndrome. Fortunately, it will magically disappear when Donald Trump does.

I finally figured it out. Trump pronounces whining as winning.

PRESIDENTIAL NICKNAME CONTEST:

Agolf Twitler
Big Baby Bunker Bitch
CarrotCaligula
CinnamonStalin
Dildo Braggins
Herr Coppertone VonPutinsbitch
Mangled Apricot Hellbeast
Mango Mussolini
Marmalade Shitgibbon
Orange Lump
President Pustule
Presidunce
Pustule-in-Chief
Rancid Cheetoface
The Tangerine Nightmare
Thundertwunt
卐 rump
TrumpleThinSkin
Twatwaffle
Tweetler-Turd
Yamhead

Hey, @realDonaldTrump: Twitter says that you have 76.4 million followers. Only 62 million Americans voted for you. My guess is that you have 20 million real voters, 6 million foreigners who can't vote, 50 million bots, and 400,000 Putin supporters.

If Trump loses the support of America's oligarchs, he'll be forced to make a run for Moscow.

Make Trump pay for his crimes? I'll go to law school if necessary.

One thing that makes me furious about Trump is that he picks on the weakest: immigrants fleeing war, Native Americans simply trying to survive, women who he can assault because they have no power next to his battery of soulless lawyers. But when he gets next to dangerous and evil human beings like Vladimir Putin and Kim Jon Il, he kisses their asses.

One thing we'll learn is how depraved Trump's oldest sons are... it will be like Uday and Qusay, but with no excuses for living in a desert.

Sadly, with Donald Trump in charge, every day in America is April Fool's Day.

Save millions of lives. Arrest Trump now.

The president *is* the plague.

There is no ceiling to Trump's insanity nor a basement to his depravity.

There is no scientific evidence that chloroquine cures or treats the Coronavirus. However, chloroquine *can* cause your hair to yellow and make it look like a dead badger is sitting on top of your head.

Trump is the YellowStreamMedia.

Trump knew that the Coronavirus was coming. He lied. People died.

Trump lies like the rug on his big fat head.

Trump logic: If you deny that you paint your face orange long enough, no one will believe that you paint your face orange.

Trump loves escaping diseases. In the Vietnam War, he escaped STDs. The Coronavirus is his Iraq War.
Trump *must* go to jail.

Trump probably won't get Covid-1. He's the poster boy for the Swine Flu.

Trump should buy Greenland so he can live there with all of his supporters and never be faced with the truth from the media again. Win-win for everyone! Except for Greenlanders.

Trump, The Stochastic Terrorist.

Trump: America's biggest loser.

Trump? Now I know what it's like to be held hostage by the criminals in Home Alone.

Trump's forcing meat plants to stay open makes this a great time to consider veganism.

Trump's getting revenge on every woman who turned him down, every man who is smarter than him, and a country that is too good for him.

Trump's *only* concern? The stock market and how it might affect his reelection chances.

#TrumpVirus.

Under Trump, every day is a new Benghazi, but with 750 to 1,000 deaths a day, rather than just four. Sadly, that's still all good to Trump supporters.

Unfortunately, we've learned that when the senate is owned by the president, America loses.

Unless Trump is defeated on November 3, you'll see how closely Trump follows Putin, and it won't be pretty.

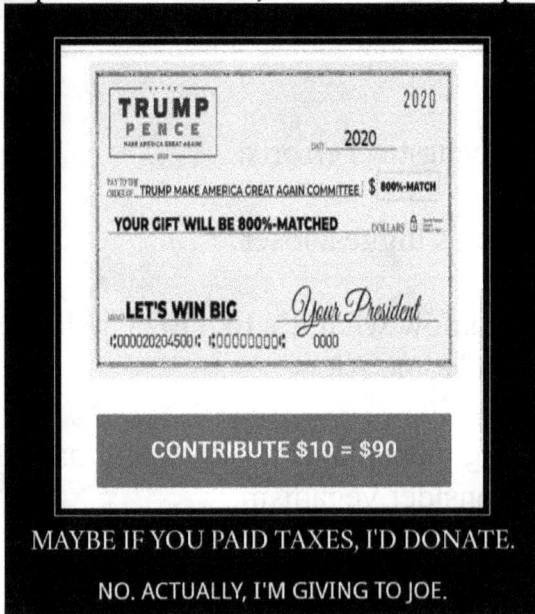

2 Random Ridiculousness

Cfku Tpmru

I miss the days when people looked up to America.

If there is a Deep State, it had better get its ass in gear soon.

I've heard that Trump's been toast for years. Show me the toaster.

Cards Against Humanity isn't a party game. It's a road map to understanding the Trump administration.

Facebook needs a new identifying icon that designates people who are not American citizens and can't vote. It would save *so* much time.

Fake news is a term Trump stole from Adolf Hitler.

I hate it when people from other countries assume that I voted for Trump because I'm an American. I don't assume that everyone in Britain voted for Bore Us Johnson.

People like Claudia Conway and Caroline Rose Giuliani give me hope. The Kids Are All Right!

I hate Twitter, but I realize that it's the perfect record of all of the evidence that will put Trump in prison... at the very least.

I have no car, so I can't drive anyone to the polls this November, but I *can* trip older Trump supporters who are walking to the polls.

I need TP for my bunghole! Rubles should work.

Donald Trump is the greatest leader that Russia has ever had.

I no longer trust people who have the American flag shown prominently in their Facebook profile pics. They invariably love Trump more than they love America.

I was taught to fear Russia and China, then Vietnam, Iran and North Korea, when all along I should have feared my own president.

I was vomiting and sick to my stomach all day yesterday. I don't think that I have the Coronavirus. I think I've just seen too many images of Donald Trump and Mike Pence lately.

I went into my bank today wearing a mask and carrying a note demanding $1 million. I was arrested. I told the SWAT officers that I was only being sarcastic, so they let me go.

If I was afraid to go to the store without a gun, I wouldn't buy a gun. I'd go to a different store.

If you're over 40 in America and you're not a millionaire, America doesn't need you.

In the Time of Trump I drink so as not to implode.

It always raises one of my eyebrows when someone asks, Don't you ever sleep? How can *anyone* sleep through the Trump Clusterfuck?

I'm kind of a big deal. Me and Donald and Leona, we don't pay taxes. That's for the little people. Like you.

It's never really been funny, this Trump nightmare. It's like Ed Wood directing a slapstick comedy with ghouls and death and liars as the movie's stars and a budget of $1,200.

I received my $1,200 check in the mail today from the government. I took it to the bank. They would not accept it. The money was in rubles.

If we get November 3, 2020 right, we can all stay and rebuild America.

If you are a captive, no matter how kind your owner, you're still a slave.

If you haven't been fired or insulted by Donald Trump, well, that's two of us!

Someone congratulated me on my upcoming comedy show, saying "Have fun and knock them dead." - I said, "Only the Republicans."

If your child spelled hamburger as hamberder, coffee as Covfefe, unprecedented as unpresidented, counsel as councel, border as boarder and Marine Corps as Marine core, would you still blame his teachers... even if your son was 73 years old?

If you're a governor and care about your citizens, you may have to suck up to Trump right now. Come November? Trump's going to jail.

Gee, if I'd known that you were a felon Trump fan who can't vote, I wouldn't have wasted my time arguing with you!

"Do these troglodyte Facebook MAGA trolls wear special protective gloves to keep their knuckles from being chafed when they drag them on the ground?" - Scot Gassen

I hate it when a Supreme Court justice steals my best defense: "I like beer!"

Kellyanne Conway: Alternative Human.

I'm sure glad that Coronavirus is just a Democratic hoax.

It's sudden-death overtime in Game 7 of the Stanley Cup Finals, and your team needs a goal to win. You're in the opponent's zone and you have the puck with only a few seconds left in the second overtime period. Your team has a man advantage because an opponent is serving the last few seconds of a tripping penalty. You don't have a clear shot at the goal, but your teammate is wide open at the side of the net and a passing lane is open. You don't really like that particular teammate, so you take a shot, it ricochets off the opposing team's defenseman, past you and out across the blue line. The opponent with the tripping penalty is just stepping out of the penalty box, so he takes the loose puck in on your goaltender with a breakaway. Goal! He scores! Your team loses. All because you didn't like your teammate... Joe Biden.

Looks like it will be strictly online dating for the next year or two.

Neither Hillary Clinton nor Joe Biden would have disbanded the pandemic team, cried every few minutes on Twitter, allowed corporations to dump sludge in our waterways, allowed oil drilling in sacred Native American lands, or continued active genocide against Native Americans.

Pick a side. A future, or Trump.

There's no liberal antidote to Fox News because honesty and integrity is not news, it's simply expected.

They're making a movie about the 2020 presidential election and the Republican party. It's called: There Will Be Cheating.

Things look bleak, but there *has* to be a resistance plan in the works by the deep state - people like me and you who won't surrender America to dictatorship. Keep heart.

This may sound crazy, but I believe that America is in the middle of WWIII and is fighting against itself for its very soul.

Today I kept busy during my self-isolation. I went through 40 bags of Cheetos looking for one that looked like Donald Trump.

Donald Trump turned me into a socialist for just $1,200.

One of the coolest things about Trumpsters & Traitors 1 and 2 is that people buy copies to troll their own relatives!

"Conservatives" want to rape the earth of its last riches. What are they conserving?

Funny how things change. Liberals are now the true conservatives.

November 3, 2020. I vote once again. November 4, 2020? All bets are off.

I've been waiting for George Soros to pay up for three years now.

When I was studying in college in the late 1970s and early '80s, most of my classes were challenging and interesting. When and where, exactly, did the dumbing down of America begin? And who benefited?

I post against Trump so as not to implode.

There is no due process when Mark Zuckerberg's minions send you to Facebook Jail. Stay under the radar.

Music, nature and laughter - all are gifts from God, as well as natural antidotes to Trumpism.

I think that America needs a long and deep look at free speech and what it really means.

I'm no Nostradamus, but I've never wavered since Trump came down that stupid escalator.

I regret that I have but one Facebook profile to give for my country.

We need to win by such a margin in 2020 that when Trump cries, *"Fake News!"* - and he will - everyone will laugh at him.

I never needed an assault weapon. My penis size is fine.

I remember the days when I only heard from the president of the United States when there was something important to be said. I miss those days. Bigly.

Most of us look back at the Salem Witch Trials with a mix of disbelief and sadness. That's how sane people will look back upon the Trump years.

I'd nuke a hurricane before I'd vote for Donald Trump.

I am such a dummy. I invested in Bic pens when I should have invested in Newell's Sharpies. Trump's free advertising is making investors billions and billions and billions.

Some might say that mocking the Trump administration is a revolutionary act. I say that it's a requirement.

Remember when you could get in a fist fight and walk away as friends because it wasn't about politics? I miss those days.

Miss America has always been beautiful. I miss America.

I remember feeling badly for Russians in college, when they only had two main news outlets, Pravda and Izvestia.

Reading a story about Japanese soldiers not surrendering after WWII oddly reminds me of Donald Trump after November 3.

I hate to repeat myself, but I will always be proud to say, "Fuck Trump!"

It seems specifically weird that 64 percent of Americans love my jokes and 36 percent hate them.

I try to share non-political posts as much as possible, but every time I do, it feels like I'm giving Donald Trump a pass.

I'm shocked. I thought Michael Bolton was doing a pretty good job.

When turnover at your workplace exceeds 75 percent, it's probably not all the employees' fault.

I'm no fan of Todd Palin, but... that voice alone...

Coal miners, farmers and other traditionally rural communities went with Trump, bigly. After nearly four horrendous years, it's actually harming them in ways that they can see.

I used to feel bad about not having a job, but then I learned about the Trump family.

Everything is possible when you're a pathological liar.

Trump accusing Mike Pompeo of not working hard enough to find Hillary's emails is like Mike Pompeo accusing Donald Trump of never catching Ronald McDonald's Hamburglar.

Jess Dweck ✓
@TheDweck

Not important but why does he sit on every chair like it's a toilet

DEPENDS...

WWII. When fighting fascism was cool.

Marked safe from energy-efficient light bulb attacks.

The wheels of justice move slowly. When it comes to Donald Trump, it feels like the wheels don't turn at all.

No sleep till indictments and incarceration.

May the men and women of the U.S. military who support Trump wake up before November 3, 2020.

Trump? I've only just begun to fight.

Melania Trump used to have normal eyes. Having too much money leads to nutty decisions.

I blame the Trump University Electoral College for America's last three nightmare years.

Cruising around with Leslie, a woman dressed in orange prison garb and wearing an oversized Donald Trump mask at an anti-Trump demonstration in downtown San Diego in 2019 was a blast. She would give a thumbs up and say, "Bigly, or Covfefe!" I'd add, "Notice the tiny hands!" Literally hundreds of people took pictures of her, laughing. I soon realized that this was probably the best marketing opportunity that I could ask for, and Leslie started holding up my book and promoting it to the crowd. Good time$!

Pathetic polls purposely put Putin's pick past people, putting pedophile past political parties & patriots.

Trump *should* be fiction. Unfortunately, he's not, and we have to solve him.

People love to complain about small errors in movies, which are fiction by their very nature, but somehow miss the fiction that Trump was "elected."

America is the Titanic. Trump is the iceberg. Republican politicians are the rats leaving the sinking ship. Most

Democratic politicians are sleeping through the sinking. American citizens are locked below decks in third class.

I've got an idea. In return for receiving the Nobel Peace Prize, Trump then immediately resigns along with Pence, and the $1 million prize money goes to Planned Parenthood. Thoughts?

My teachers failed me. They never showed me where in the Constitution it says that presidents are required to suck up to their favorite dictators.

Some people say, "Fuck Trump!" Wags say, "With Pence's wife's dick!"

Recently, a walrus defending its young sunk a Russian landing craft in the Arctic. No word on whether John Bolton sustained any injuries.

Attorney General Bill Barr is looking a bit orange at the gills lately. I think that he's been under Trump's light bulbs a little too long.

Very pleased to say that my doctor says I'm finally free of windmill cancer!

WHEN YOU'RE GAY

BUT NOT HAPPY

Old white men try to discredit Greta Thunberg, saying that she's an actor. Apparently, they've completely forgotten Ronald Reagan.

Mocking stupidity is free speech.

Most people are pretty cool about not reading what's on your laptop or phone screen when you're at a cafe or bar or airport. That's why I enjoy writing my anti-Trump jokes in public.

I don't believe a word that anyone in the Trump administration says. Until they're out of the Trump administration. And then I believe about one word they say... because they were *in* the Trump administration at one point.

I can take jokes about Barack Obama and Hillary Clinton. Why can't Trump supporters take a joke about Trump?

I've discovered the solution to Trump. Simply have yourself cryogenically frozen until he's gone.

If he thinks Hillary's emails are in the Ukraine, Trump's insane and his brain is down the drain.

In the time of Trump, sleep is a luxury.

People think that Trump calls Mike Pence "VP Pence." But he actually is saying "Pee Pee Pence."

The best-selling new children's book is "Pee Pee Pence," by I.P. Frehly.

Tax those earning more than $1 million a year at least 50 percent. Pay the homeless to collect cans, clean streets and alleys, and in return, please give them roofs over their heads. Make becoming a "millionaire" something worth achieving.

Bernie Sanders is a wonderful human being with a huge heart. It's no wonder that the Trump presidency gave him a heart attack.

Trump suggesting that China investigate Joe Biden assumes that China wants Trump to stay in office.

I'll vote a ham sandwich before I'll vote for a Republican. (Dead or alive.)

Trump said the only reason he made the Ukrainian call was Rick Perry asked him something about natural gas. Perry's question was: "Who farted?"

I'm dreaming of a pale garbage Christmas!

Trump ages like a fine whine.

Try these Trump defenses the next time you're in trouble:

"Yes, I gave the bank teller a note telling her to fill a bag with money, but I was just kidding."

"Sure, I said I'd like to date my own daughter, but look how hot she is!"

"I'd like to pay my taxes, but they're being audited, so I can't."

WORLD'S GREATEST LIAR

If Donald Trump was drowning, I'd run and get the biggest glass of water I could find.

I miss my parents, but I'm very grateful that they didn't have to live through this era of the Orange Shitgibbon.

Breaking News: "Ivanka Trump gifted 18 trademarks in China including one for voting machines." Ivanka Votink Machinks!

If our nation's courts and security agencies don't stop the Trump march to fascism soon, it may soon be time to go underground, Fahrenheit 451 style.

If Trump was on fire, I'd run and find a package of hot dogs to grill.

Several people on Facebook have posted that Kellyanne Conway is the whistleblower inside the White House. She may blow someone's whistle, but otherwise, that's the dumbest thing I've heard in weeks.

Demanding only civil criticism of Donald Trump is like asking Nazis not to wear their swastikas on Sundays.

Gallows humor is making a big comeback.

You know that America is in trouble when cognitive dissonance is stronger than reverence for the Constitution.

I've met many Navy personnel who don't vote as a matter of perverse personal pride. So, they permit their peers who *do* vote to control their lives...and ours.

I'm starting a new rock and roll band: Pale Garbage!

Trump discussions in public? First, I feel people out. When I find out which way they lean, and they're Trumpsters, that's the end of the conversation. If they're patriots, we commiserate with each other.

WHEN ALIEN DNA
WEARS OUT

Trump? So much stupidity, so little time.

Trump attacks Mexicans, Muslims, children he cages, blacks, judges who oppose him, Gold Star parents, the two or three Republicans who don't kiss his ass, Democrats, etc. Eventually, it's going to be your turn. Why not wake up now and join true patriots and fight against Trump's American fascism? Our parties are way better than Trump rallies - we have alcohol, dancing and great rock & roll. You have opioids, ugly red hats and Ted Nugent.

Mocking Trump at this late date is like singing drunkenly as the American Titanic sinks into history.

I truly believe that America will flush Trump and once again be a beacon of freedom to the world. Unfortunately, my optimism often overrules my common sense.

Bone spurs. Never forget the power of bone spurs.

Trump is obviously oblivious to his crimes. Lock him up and teach him the errors of his ways.

Real estate companies who put "TRUMP" on their buildings are feeling contrite. As their structures empty and their profits shrink, they're now dropping the first two letters and replacing them with CH.

Had I known that Robert Mueller would waste a year of my life because of a fucking memo, I'd have concentrated on making money.

Saturday Night Live doesn't always tell the truth. Why not? Because it's satire, you moron!

I've got guts! I'm going thrill-seeking in a rural area... wearing a TAN suit!

I am marshaling my arguments against Trump. Give me 500 years.

> "It vas the vest of times, it vas the vorst of times." - Moronia Trump

Jail to the Chief!

The ridiculous historical arguments that I hear from many Americans my own age make me understand that these people never again cracked a book about history once they had slept through their high school years.

Free speech? That's only for Trump on Twitter.

Keep yourself alive. Trumpism *will* be defeated.

I wonder how many abortions Donald Trump has paid for?

If Republicans stop lying about open borders and abortion, Democrats will stop telling the truth about Republicans and treason. Deal?

I never knew what gaslighting was before the Russians installed Trump. It's a helluva thing to have to learn about from a "president."

Trump and his enablers are scared. And therefore dangerous.

I'm about to crash. Let me check Twitter and see the latest moronic missive from Ms. Donald.

If Ivanka weren't Trump's daughter, perhaps I'd be dating her.

Twitter stopped accepting political ads? Cool! Now ban Trump.

I understand that Trump thinks we're stupid enough to believe his staged "situation room" photos... but are his generals?!

Did you hear about the Trump supporter who got in trouble with the law? He said, "I'm making a run for the border." A friend said, "Mexico?" "No," said the scofflaw. "Colorado."

We all need a good Facebook alternative. Wouldn't *that* chap Fuckerberg's ass?!

Remember when Devin Nunes sued an imaginary cow? Good times!

I'm going to start a new rock band. The Intolerant Liberals.

Jane Fonda recently was arrested four weeks in a row, fighting against climate change. In the same time period, Melania Trump had four pedicures.

The House of Cads is crumbling. (Pun intended.)

I want my county back.

One cool thing about being banned on Facebook? While you can't post anything, "like" anything, or use Facebook Messenger, you *can* report haters and losers (Trumpsters) all day long. Use this backdoor tool that I've discovered (I call it the "Matt Gaetz Portal"), and #resist getting completely "Zucked."

No one's coming to save us. Certainly not the Democratic candidates. Only we can save the USA.

People say Kellyanne Conway or Mike Pence might be the whistleblower. I laugh heartily. No way.

I'm starting to like Trump's strategy. Just yell at everyone I don't like and refuse to participate. I used to pay my taxes, but now I think that I'll just walk away and forget about them. Thanks, Don the Con!

Charles Lee "Chucky" Ray is all grown up and now calls himself Donald J. Trump.

As to Trump's wall, people forget that they can get tools at Home Depot to cut through that damn thing... Not to mention Mexican jumping human beings.

Russia? North Korea? Turkey? Trump only learns from the worst.

America will never heal until the boil that is Trump is finally excised from America's rump.

On October 17, 2018, New York City had its first weekend without a shooting in 25 Years. Donald Trump apparently wasn't on 5th Avenue.

I just discovered the best soundtrack for reading about Donald Trump's impeachment: Animals, by Pink Floyd.

I pulled an all-nighter before the impeachment hearings so that I didn't sleep through history. Impeach Trump!

AOC has guts. Trump has no nuts.

Chuck Woolery claims that supporting Trump ruined his career. I've seen his tweets. He's a wimpy cross between crazy James Woods and a crying Scott Baio.

Republicans are losing elections, dropping out of politics, or being arrested for crimes. The swamp is self-cleaning!

I miss the days when the Steele Dossier said, "Donald Trump, Urine Trouble."

OK. I admit it. I am the whistleblower.

Trump is above the law! He's protecting the slim white majority from the brown hordes who earn their money by their blood and sweat and don't even care about the stock market, dividends or even offshore accounts! They're barbarians! They don't pay for scalp tightening, Botox, nose and boob jobs to make themselves look more presentable!

Working our asses off, we ignored politics, focusing on our careers, dreams and families, then politicians we elected sold us out.

To save America, you must marry: Sarah H. Sanders, Kellyanne Conway, Jeanine Pirro, Stephen Miller, Eric Trump or Devin Nunes. Go!

What is Trump afraid of? He's afraid of us knowing that he cheats on his taxes, how much he owes to Putin, and the secret patent for his hair "style."

Selfish, I know, but one of the worst things about the Trump presidency is how Lindsey Graham tarnished my surname.

After Trump, I will never take a politician for granted again.

My newest and favorite insult: "That's perhaps the dumbest thing that Trump hasn't yet said."

> **DAMN OBAMA! IF HE'D TAKEN A THIRD TERM, NONE OF THIS SHIT WOULD HAVE HAPPENED.**

Money will eventually be Trump's downfall. Imagine him on the run, grabbing gold bars from Fort Knox and stuffing them in his fat suit's pockets. Then falling off a boat taking him into hiding... he has the gold bars, but to survive, he must shed his suitcoat and the gold bars or drown. First, how can the out-of-shape fatso get his jacket off in time, and, second, do you really think that he'd let go of the gold bars?

Marie Yovanovitch, an American ambassador, working to protect America and Ukraine from Russian aggression, is attacked by our "president." It's a shame and a sin, and I believe, treason on the part of Donald Trump.

Everyone smart enough to know that Don the Con is evil is a Never Trumper.

I used to read several books a week, but I think that Trump requires constant surveillance.

Freedom fighters are on a roll, and history is on our side. America was born by breaking away from tyranny.

Political office... the last refuge to which a Republican scoundrel clings.

I would like to thank all of the women and men who have served our country honorably without growing bonespurs.

The Trump administration is like an incredibly funny and horrifying comedy... that's true life!

Once Trump is gone, I hope we can get back to sleeping at night, reading books and worrying about who's going to win on Survivor.

Trump will be America's shame forever, just like Hitler is Germany's.

Trump's next job: License Plate Maker.

Trump tried a Google search but he spelled it Gooble and got lost in Internet hell.

Not allowed to run a casino *or* a charity! That's the kind of man I can trust to run my country!

Putin's Desires, 2016, Fulfilled:
A. Trump gets elected.
B. Americans fight amongst each other.
C. Republican politicians take bribes to ensure their loyalty to Trump (Putin).

You say Melanoma, I say Moronia, let's call the whole thing off.

Denial... a river in Egypt that has infected the Trump administration.

I've met some incredible American patriots in Facebook jail.

Trump is on top for now, but things change.

Remember the video showing Donald Trump and Jeffrey Epstein "bopping" to cheerleaders dancing at a party? Add up all of those girls' brain cells and you come up with Ivanka's IQ.

Why does Melania Trump squint? Because it makes everything look bigger.

Shepard Smith, Keith Olbermann, whomever... it doesn't matter what network you are on, telling the truth will get you fired.

If you and I were billionaires, many of the world's problems would disappear. Billionaires are not the problem. Greed is.

I don't write dystopian novels because I don't want to give people like Donald Trump and other terrorists ideas.

Love America? Vote Blue. Love Russia, vote Red, Green, Independent or just stay home... same fucking thing.

Make Trump Get a Real Job for Once.

Why does Trump want to lower standards on water pressure and say we're flushing the toilet 10 to 15 times? Hamberders and Freedom Fries.

What does Donald Trump call 7:40 a.m.? "Twenty to hate."

Liars used to be looked down upon. Now they're in charge of America.

If I've hurt you and you didn't deserve it, I apologize. If I've hurt you and you're a Trump voter, you're welcome.

The entire world needs a safe place from Trump.

Ted Cruz defends Trump, the man who claimed that Cruz's father helped killed JFK. Have we hit bottom yet?

The geographic center of the contiguous United States is Lebanon, Kansas. Just like Trump's mind, there's nothing there.

Nancy Pelosi says she doesn't hate Donald Trump. I respect that. I don't hate Nazis, white supremacists or liver.

If the bar exam is so difficult, why are there so many lawyers in Congress?

A ham sandwich would defeat Trump in a fair election.

I'm the Deep State Brewery. What'll y'all have?

I got into the U.S. on an Einstein Bagels visa.

What does Melania Trump say when Donald gets it up once a year? "Vinning!"

I never go outside anymore because of windmill cancer and unpresidented covfefe.

"I flushed 15 times once.
That frickin' last kilo of Adderall
just.
Would.
Not.
Flush."
- Donald Trump

I never thought much about the U.S. Supreme Court until I saw a traitor stack it.

Vladimir Putin only gave me $2 to sell out my country. That's $2 more than George Soros gave me, though!

When the "president" of the United States shouldn't be the leader of F-Troop, let alone the free world.

I'm an American citizen who is seeing everything that I love disparaged and dying. That's why I fight Trump.

Donald Trump is as nutty as a hatter. (Sorry, hatters.)

I'm tired of paying taxes to subsidize Vladimir Putin's extravagant lifestyle.

Some civilizations have died for much simpler reasons than a lack of morality. Lack of water, for instance. The American civilization is dying because of an excess of greed.

Let's see if I've got this straight: Rudy Giuliani got an American ambassador to Ukraine fired to obstruct a real investigation of Russian election meddling so he could pursue a fake investigation of Ukrainian election meddling?

America as an institution is way stronger than a few thousand big-talking cowards.

I'm OK. I'm just sad. I'm getting older. Friends are dying. Trump is surviving. Ya know?

Putin is evil and intelligent. Trump is evil and moronic.

If we can't trust Facebook, who can we trust? Mwahahaha!!!!

My sense of injustice is strong. Probably too strong. Having a mentally ill racist as "president" sure isn't helping.

Lindsey Graham and Mitch McConnell are starving and you have two sandwiches. Do you eat both sandwiches for lunch, or do you save one for dinner?

Independents? Ha! In what universe? There are Dems, Repubs and the apathetic or brain dead.

The Republicans are not playing a game. They're playing for life and death. Dems must, too.

Would you rather have never learned who your Trump-supporting friends are, or the truth as you now know it?

No one has attacked me for saying "Merry Christmas" and I can't believe it. Guess I have to give Trump props!

The post-impeachment civil war has begun. I was in line at Walmart and a woman cut in front of me.

A work-around so you don't get a Facebook jail sentence: *"Not See."* ™

"Chris Christie wades into Senate impeachment fight." - MSN News. "Sea levels rise to tsunami levels." - Me

Sorry that I haven't been around for a while. I've been busy raking local forests.

Breaking News: "Lindsey Graham Fills Up Dirigible with Just His Hot-Flash Vapors! Yet, there was still danger of a huge explosion!"

I swear, Trump supporters post on social media just to prove that they can type. Not spell. Type.

Billionaire Trump supporters received a return on their investment. Average Americans received a steel-toed boot to the teeth... with no commensurate health care.

Ben Carson is in the dictionary under "Pathetic."

What does Trump's existence prove? That big mouths are an evolutionary advantage?

Donald Trump did one wonderful thing for me. He completely cleaned up my Facebook friends list.

Survival of the fittest in America? It's when guys like Trump with $400 million inheritances are considered tough.

When I think of the Trump administration at Christmas, I think of ho, ho, ho, ho...

I think that I know what is killing the birds. Windmill cancer!

Wind turbines kill birds. Cars kill birds. Planes kill birds. Let's ban 'em all and use more coal. But only the clean kind!

Trump's hair? It's a special nonflammable fabric made only in Moscow.

Donald Trump's umbrella protects Melania from rain like the Constitution protects us from Donald Trump.

Yep. He's beyond stupid. But he's *our* dictator! Yay! (Laughing to keep from crying.)

"Tell a horror story with just one word and one number." Shiro Ken. "Reelected 2020." - Me

I'm a proud liberal. I may or may not own guns. Any Trumpian who attacks me or mine is going to have to guess.

Someone said, "Live every day as if it were your last." I said, "Every day under Trump feels like my last."

Something will happen. The floodgates will open. America is better than this.

You could block Satan on Facebook, and someone would shame you for not being open to other viewpoints.

Happy 2020. Let's evict the Orange Blob!

It's 2020. It's got to be better than the last four years! Right?

I've got the world's greatest political joke! It's *Donald Trump*!

I've never been all that great, but Trump has made me much worse.

Anyone but Trump. Even Satan had a conscience.

I used to have a bad opinion of revolutionaries.

I'm all in against Trump. I'll take that bet. I'd rather lose than be an enabler of American fascism.

A friend said Trump was finally toast, considering the news that Michael Duffey, a White House official, ordered the hold on military assistance to Ukraine 90 minutes after Trump's July 2019 phone call with Zelensky. Trump's been "toast" so many times that America should have an extreme bread shortage.

Pathetic knows no nationalism.

I'm starting a new military force: The Bone Spurs Brigade. Our battle flag will be white with a yellow stripe on the back.

Let's get that beer, see that concert, spend that money and live for today. With Trump, there's no guarantee of a tomorrow.

Trump's Greatest Hits:

Build an Imaginary Wall!

Space Farce! Ban a Religion!

Taxes are Only for the Poor!

If You're Brown, You're Down!

If You're White, You're Right!

If You're Dumb, You're My Kinda Bum!

For my 4th of July meal, I had Chinese food handed to me over the counter by a Mexican in a strip mall owned by a Portuguese. My flag was made in Myanmar and my fishing pole in Japan. America's strength is its inclusiveness. Happy 4th of July! 🩶

Being right about Trump gives no satisfaction.

The Selective Service website crashed because it was overwhelmed by people fearing the return of a military draft. Yay, Trump!

Asking me if I'd book a room at a Trump Tower is like a doctor asking if you'd like a colonoscopy without sedation.

You can love America and hate Trump. It's called patriotism and respect for the Constitution.

Almost all of my disagreements with people are based upon misunderstandings. All of my disagreements with Trump are based on complete understanding.

My fears about G.W. Bush were about 15 on a scale of 1 to Donald Trump.

I'd have a lot more friends if I didn't express strong opinions against Trump, but then I'd self-implode out of a lack of self respect.

What'll it take? Trump burning books? Certain U.S. citizens wearing arm bands? Or not until he comes for you?

Trump will eventually target American libraries, but he'll leave Netflix alone.

People remain friends despite my anti-Trump rants. They're afraid that I might become president. It's not farfetched. Trump did.

Since guns keep us safe, please allow them at Republican conventions and Trump rallies.

Putin's agents may have missed me, but I'm convinced that they've influenced Trump supporters.

You're elected president in 2020 and you're name is not Trump. What are your first 10 priorities? Go!

We're laughing to keep from strangling.

Remember, we didn't learn until after he was dead that Hitler had been pumped full of drugs by his doctor...

Something besides his 35 percent is propping Donald Trump up. (Putin!) Excuse me.

None of the fuckers who Trump has fired care enough for America to strangle him before quitting.

Corporations have free speech. Workers responsible for corporate profits? Manure has better resale value.

Know how billionaires became billionaires? Off the backs of rubes. What rubes? You and me.

You know how billionaires keep saying that they should be taxed more? Why wait for the government? Give some money to the needy now, you greedy pricks.

In 2016, Melania Trump threatened to sue anyone claiming she used to be a hooker. Can we call her a current hooker?

Even after nearly four years of Trump, every time I find out that someone I care about is a Trump supporter, it's still like a punch in the gut.

If I wanted to be a dictator, I'd surround myself with yes men, denigrate the rule of law, and incite the moronic.

You're already dealing with Trump, and then termites attack your home. WTF, universe?

I've met thousands of people from around the world during my life. The ones I'm still in touch with ask me how the hell Trump happened.

Here's an idea for an American war: How about a war on termites? It's one I'm sure that we can win!

I need to take a break from Facebook, but I fear that if I take a day off, Trump will nuke California.

When Mike Pence is indicted, Trump will say, "I don't know the gentleman. I take photos with everybody."

Whiteaboutism. It's a uniquely American version of a Russian propaganda technique.

Anyone but Trump. Putin loves one-candidate voters.

What do I think of when I hear "The Big Easy"? Melania Trump.

Marked safe from Bowling Green Massacre, Ebola and Jade Helm.

It's mind boggling how pedophiles became the rulers of America. I did Nazi that coming.

Satan is better than Trump. At least *he* fulfills his promises.

This morning, I asked a San Diego sailor: "What are you going to do if Trump gives you an illegal order?" "Oh, that's a tough one," he said. I said, "No. It's an easy one. A fucking easy one."

Why could we see Al Capone's taxes and not Trump's? They're both criminals.

The National Enquirer is to news as Donald Trump is to honesty.

Looking for positives about Trump, I came up with this: He fired a lot of assholes that he hired.

You took a break from Trump news to save your sanity? The bad news is simply multiplied by the number of days you took off.

I'm not as worried about the Coronavirus as I am the Moscow Treason Virus, which was transmitted directly from Moscow to Trump's White House in 2016.

I don't watch horror movies. They remind me too much of the Trump administration.

So that I don't live in a political bubble, I allow one designated Republican to troll my Facebook posts.

I can't believe the courage of people who fight tyranny and have something to lose. I've got nothing to lose and I'm nervous.

Kamala Harris turned me into a newt!

- Donald Trump

"I Got Better."

It's better to be considered impolite than polite when those demanding good manners are fascists.

Greed, faux Christianity and flag waving are the three main tenets of Trumpism. Guns added for flavor.

A feeling of invincibility comes before a big fall. (Or a big thump, like when you get hit in the rump by a stump, Trump.)

There's a Manhattan in Kansas. Don't tell Trump. He might bomb it!

Trump's going to go off. Think he's done crazy shit? You haven't seen anything yet.

I'm no detective, but I am guessing that someone has compromising material on Alan Dershowitz, Lindsey Graham and others in the Trump administration.

I'm shocked at how many people point fingers at Donald Trump's many crimes when Barack Obama once actually wore a *tan* suit!

Trump calls Mario Rubio "Little Marco." Now I understand why. He must have seen him at a few Jeffrey Epstein parties.

When Trumpsters sling dirt, sling shit back. Going high when they go low won't work with bullies. Try appeasing Hitler.

Republicans have won the language war ever since Newt "Salamander" Gingrich came on the scene. I think part of the problem is that 'liberal' has come to mean 'effete,' like Alan Colmes when he 'defended' the majority viewpoint in America with thick glasses and a wimpy persona. As far as I am concerned, Alan Colmes did as much damage to America as Newt Gingrich did.

I refuse to watch Trump's speeches live. I can get the lowlights on the Internet later.

I believe high school dropouts about politics like I believe Bristol Palin on celibacy.

NASA saw something come out of a black hole for the first time. The black hole was Trump's ass. What they saw coming out was Sean Hannity's head.

The only thing that could surprise me about the Trump administration is if someone in it was ever accused of telling the truth.

I just blocked Fox News from my Google news feed. Some might say that I'll live in an "echo chamber," but I'm not worried. I can still see all the fascist news that I can stomach on Facebook.

It will be interesting to see what women think of Trump once all their rights have been rolled back.

I've slowly learned that safety warnings on products apply only to the dumbest people - like Donald Trump. So, if you have half a brain, break out those lawn darts and Tide Pods!

So many words rhyme with Trump. Try a few. You can't go wrong.

The right wing has co-opted the American flag and our military, as if liberals or Democrats never fought for America.

Americans have two choices on November 3, 2020. Unfortunately, one is Damien from The Omen.

Look what tolerant liberals have allowed to happen to us: We now have the ugliest and most hateful president and administration in American history.

Asking me to be tolerant of fascism is like asking Jews to be tolerant of anti-Semitism. I'll fight to save my country.

Climate change? Don't worry about it. Only our children will suffer.

There's only one way to save America. Everyone needs to buy Donald Trump as many McDonald's gift certificates as possible.

Stochastic terrorism and gaslighting? Trump's modus operandi.

Trump didn't come to drain the swamp. He came to drain the *U.S. Treasury.*

Trump's Enemies List is going to make Nixon's look like a birthday-party invitation list.

We've been to the moon. Trump doesn't want to go to the moon to learn anything or to colonize it. He wants to go to the moon so that he can brag about it.

The Earth is perfect. The moon is dead like Trump's heart.

With Trump in charge, act like every minute is your last. It just might be.

I've been a juror four more times than Trump has been bankrupt.

You think *you* are sick of my political posts?! Get rid of Trump and I'll shut up. If Trump stays, I stay. Your choice.

YouTube, the loser's go-to source in a political argument.

I miss the old days, when the Russians were America's enemy and everyone agreed upon it.

It's a scientific fact that people fart more during the Trump regime than during any other presidential administration. That last fact really stinks!

Why do Trump supporters tell me to do something to myself that is physically impossible?

Covid-19 has now passed from being a pandemic to being a morondemic.

Fence sitters and earpluggers don't make the best citizens.

Which Ted Nugent song describes Trump best? Stormtroopin'.

Tik Tok? I don't care if it gets banned or if Microsoft buys it, but I *will* be pissed off if Trump makes money on the deal.

What if Donald Trump was tarred and feathered and run out of America on a rail? It is what it is.

What's the theme song for Donald Trump's fixation with Hydroxychloroquine? Steppenwolf's The Pusher.

Republicans try to shame me over my hatred of Trump. I feel a twinge of guilt, and then I think of the Obama effigies they burned, and I come to my senses and tell them to fuck off.

MCCONNELL ON CLINTON IMPEACHMENT

"I am completely and utterly perplexed by those who argue that perjury and obstruction of justice are not high crimes and misdemeanors."

SEN. MITCH MCCONNELL
(R) KENTUCKY
FEBRUARY 12, 1999

LIVE
MSNBC
7:11 PM ET

In the time of Trump, I'm beginning to second-guess pacifism.

I'm guessing that Ghislaine is going to be even less popular as a girl's name in the future.

Trumpsters loved hatin' on people to his song "Rockin' In The Free World." Now they hate Neil Young because Trump's gotta pay for a song he stole? Murica!

Saying "at least I'm not as bad as Donald Trump" sets a very low bar.

If the world wasn't laughing at America because of Donald Trump, I'd be very worried about the world.

A poor man *can* be president. Donald Trump proved it.

Which brand of chips are Trump supporters most likely to favor? Lead-based chips.

Frontline workers, no matter what their pay rate, are American heroes.

Take whatever Trump says, do the opposite, and you'll be OK.

I'll fight Trumpism, don't worry about that. I'll also annoy the enemy with jokes!

After Trump is gone, I'll only post pics of kittens and puppies, I swear!

The black guy got Bin Laden. Never forget.

America *can* be fixed. We just need to keep fighting for our beliefs and never give up. These are dark days, but hope keeps the light of freedom alive.

If Ted Nugent performs at the Republican virtual convention, I suggest that one item is more important than masks: earplugs.

Kanye? Not happening. That would mean that black people are blind to "good people on both sides," "get that son of a bitch off the field," and "there's my African American!"

Maybe Lindsey Graham isn't gay. Maybe he just hates ice cream, apple pie and fireworks!

When you place yourself above ordinary human beings... you fall.

I've got a cheap solution for everyone complaining that they can't get their hair cut: Buy a damn hat.

It's the end of the world as we know it... and I feel nauseous.

There are some things I really need to accomplish the next time I'm sober. Might be after January 20, 2021, though.

Kanye West voters are just like Kanye West. Stupid, delusional, mentally ill and manipulated.

I don't give a damn what Elon Musk says - I don't want to live on another planet.

I don't give a fuck what Trump says about Space Farce, either.

I remember how quiet and peaceful it was on my boat during the early months of the Coronavirus lockdown. How clean the water became, how the skies cleared up, how many fewer cars were polluting San Diego. Humanity may require a Coronavirus about once every few years to make us lock down and help keep our beautiful, wonderful, glorious planet alive.

Earth is a living thing, so it does have a self-preservation mechanism, as all living things do; and its arsenal is beyond our ken. If we don't take care of Mother Earth, she will take care of matters herself. Lately, she's been doing just that.

Advice for Trump supporters: Wear a mask. Wash your hands. Don't touch anyone else's face. It's not advisable that you put that gerbil up your butt.

I'd be more likely to believe in God if Coronavirus only killed racists and the greedy.

I remember learning in history classes that the Spanish Flu helped end WWII and that Spanish Fly helped kick start the War on Drugs. Abraham Lincoln wrote about those events in his iPad journal.

Trump Pimp Daddy Putin.

My guess for Kamala Harris's Trumpian nickname was Kooky Kamala. He disappointed me again.

The Trump administration will be throwing *everything* at the wall to see what sticks, all the way up to November 3... and beyond. Be ready.

Why is Trump slurring his words and having trouble drinking water from a bottle? Rhymes with Phyllis.

If Trump "wins" on November 3, he didn't win.

I know some of these Q-Anon nuts. They're evangelical know-nothings who haven't cracked open a book since the last days of high school.

Trump's insanity is as exhausting as babysitting a demonic Dennis the Menace. I hope that we all get a well-deserved rest after January 20.

You'll see... the loudest "militia men" now will be the first to run and hide if things get wild.

Let us celebrate the Statue of Liberty before Donald Trump melts her down for his wall.

Trump says Americans will have to learn Chinese if Biden is elected." - Headline."No! I've been learning Russian in case he wins a second term!" - Craig Warth

Calling a liberal a "Communist" these days is about as frightening as calling someone a "witch!"

Mike Pence's wife likes to play with her beard.

When Neil Young and Dolly Parton are against you, you're on the wrong side of history.

My neighbor is a Trumpster who claims she loves Neil Young. I turned her on to Neil's new song, "Looking for a Leader." I expect her head to explode any second now.

Donald Trump would have gone to his brother's funeral had there been money to be made.

Name *one* thing you can trust more than Donald Trump…

I had no concerns about Biden's VP pick unless it was a ham sandwich that I'd hoped to eat.

Boat Names for the Trump Administration, Edition #1

American Carnage (Putin or Trump)
Iowa Princess (Mike Pence)
Moscow Mule (Mitch McConnell)
Florida Flopper (Mario Rubio)
Canadian Cuckold (Ted Cruz)
DUI Dominator (Matt Gaetz)
Texan Tribulation (Louie Gohmert)
Grede is Gud (Betsy DeVos)
Miss Mendacious (Kayleigh McEnany)
Iowa Gasbag (Chuck Grassley)

I am Q. All Trump supporters need to go back home and stay off Facebook until I contact you with further information.

Steve Bannon making money off of a fake wall on America's southern border is like Donald Trump making money off of a fake presidency.

Trump? Same old Covfefe, different day.

Everything will be much worse if Trump is re-installed by Putin.

I could have watched the RNC Convention, but I decided to pull out my back molars with rusty pliers instead.

Third parties in America are as viable as second parties in Russia.

I remember when my parents immigrated from Hawaii and we became U.S. citizens.

Whatever you do, try not to be Trumplicit in crimes against America.

Don't worry about the asteroid that might hit the day before the election. That only happens when dinosaurs rule the Earth. Oh oh...

Making citizens who protest against extra-judicial executions your enemies is sorta like befriending dictators who hate America.

If your entire comedy act is insulting the audience, you have no act and you're not funny. However, you should consider being a speechwriter for Donald Trump.

If you're depressed and can't figure out why, it's Trump.

If the Scots ever catch the Loch Ness Monster, I anticipate this response: Loch Her Up!

I need drugs just to deal with people who supposedly don't take drugs, like Ted Nugent and Donald Trump.

A woman on Facebook used the fear of Ebola to avoid going to American hospitals. I told her that her odds of contracting Ebola in the USA are about the same as Trump being named America's greatest president.

The FBI? They're going to Jared's.

I have never known anyone, baby boy or girl, who has screamed and cried every single day of their lives... until Trump... whom I'm not sure even has a gender.

A cornered animal is never a good thing. Especially when the animal has rabies... and nukes.

A friend said that there probably isn't any truth to the theory that a chemical in McDonald's fries cure baldness, because Trump eats their food regularly. Unless, I said, if he skips the fries because they're French.

Donald Trump: You can have your military parade after every hungry child in America is assured of being fed through your term.

One thing about President Barack Obama: He knew that the office was bigger than he was.

As adult Americans, we spent our lives trying to build our careers, expecting that those we'd elected to represent us would have our best interests at heart. Boy, were *we* dumb!

One problem Donald Trump will never have: I couldn't get the laundromat's detergent out of the dispenser because my hands are too big.

It sucks to be alive just as the Second Dark Age is upon us.

Mike Pence is twisted. That's all I know for sure.

I'm watching "Highway Thru Hell." It's about truckers in bad situations, but I thought it was about the Trump administration.

Trump is Abbie Normal.

Donald Trump is the American Id, and I don't mean that as a compliment.

If, as I believe, patriotism means love of country, it also means love for your fellow American. Which means, at the very least, flushing the toilet in public restrooms.

We can't let the forces of Mordor divide us.

I'm in a deep state secret society, so I can't explain it here, but I *will* send you a memo as to why Trump is guilty as hell.

Donald Trump says more staff will leave as he seeks perfection. I don't think that the word "perfection" means what he thinks it means.

If Donald Trump is truly a billionaire, then he can easily afford $30 million for his own fucking parade.

When it comes to the environment, I am more conservative than any conservative I know.

I'm willing to testify in front of Robert Mueller without immunity. Donald?

In college, I had Iranian friends in San Diego, and then Khomeini arrived. Forty years later, I had friends all over the world, and then Trump arrived.

A looped sound bite on social media sounds like "Yanny" to some and "Laurel" to others. Funny, I hear "Impeach and Incarcerate."

Heart, soul and intelligence will always defeat evil. So I tell myself to stay alive.

I wonder what it's like to warm myself by the embers of a dying empire.

I know how to solve North Korea. Let The Donald put up a Trump Tower in Pyongyang.

I am very unhappy about the protests in England and Scotland against Trump. They are more pro-American than some American "patriots!"

Conservatives are the only people who work hard for their money.

Never trust anyone who's never left home for their thoughts about international relations.

THE TRUMP REGIME

2017-2021

I'm a writer with no experience in nuclear physics. I should be Trump's science adviser.

Donald Trump is happy that Irma is a "hericane," because he wants to reach out and grab her.

Donald Trump is insane. Rebuttals?

Most of us are just trying to get through life. Then Trump got shat upon us, and now we have to deal with that crap, too.

The Trump administration is like the worst horror film ever made, and the rest of us are all acting in it against our will.

In a just world, Trump permitting healthcare providers not to cover preexisting conditions would bite him in his ample ass.

It's an absolute disgrace that a fat blimp flew over London in Air Force One.

Donald Trump cheats at golf. But to give him credit. He gives Melania free strokes.

Donald Trump is the Kim Jong-un of Putins.

I can almost guarantee that Donald Trump's mother never told him: "If you can't say something nice, don't say anything at all."

I wish that Donald Trump, the president of Moronia, would learn how to spell, purchase Spellcheck, hire a copy editor or just STFU.

The Trump administration is like F-Troop except that things don't turn out as well in the end.

Paul Ryan said that Trump makes knee-jerk decisions. Trump said that Ryan is weak, ineffective and stupid. It's the first time I've ever agreed with either of them.

RE TAR

TED!

Every Trump supporter can honestly say, "I'm not racist; I have black friends." Yeah. Diamond and Silk.

Honest question: "What argument could a Trump supporter make to change my mind about what I can see with my own eyes?"

Wondering where Kellyanne Conway learned the phrase "many people are saying," considering she was shilling for Ted Cruz before throwing any integrity she might have had away by working for Trump. Which leads one to the natural conclusion that Trump defenders are insane.

Prison Andrew. Too soon?

I don't know if Jeffrey Epstein was murdered or committed suicide. I don't know who murdered him if he *was* murdered. I do know that William Barr ain't gonna do shit about it.

Occasionally, I look at what Trump supporters are saying in his defense in the comments section of CNN, ABC or NBC online stories. And I think, free speech has gotten out of hand.

Isn't it better to shame Nazis online than to have to fight them on the streets?

Frustrate a fascist, buy my books.

The little horse that Roy Moore rode in on to vote? It's only 13 in human years.

I remember the great and fun high-school dances we had on Friday nights, listening to Foghat's "Slow Ride," Santana's "Evil Woman," and Bachman Turner Overdrive's "Takin' Care of Business." And I wasn't in my 30s, like Roy Moore, either...

Who was Roy Moore's favorite Brady Bunch character? Cindy, of course.

In Stephen Miller, it's as if Republicans purposefully picked the ugliest person, in appearance and soul, to be the voice of America to the world.

In future dictionaries, "hypocrisy" will be a synonym for "Republican."

Omarosa. Spell it and use it in a sentence: O.M.A.R.O.S.A. - Oh My, A Ridiculous Outrage Says Adios.

Guys at a bar in arguing over the merits of Super Bowl commercials. No wonder Trump is president.

Now that some of them have seen through Donald Trump, it's unfair to paint all Republicans with a broad brush. We must use words that describe Trump supporters more specifically: Toothless Trumptards, crazy cultists, armed ammosexuals, cowardly clods, ridiculous racists, misogynistic morons, insane idiots, etc.

Trumpsters bitch about dumb people in California, not realizing how much smarter the state would be if they just moved out.

Trump fanatics searching through my previous posts and attack me with one in which I said that Robert Mueller would help finally bring Trump to justice. I neglected to mention that the U.S. Congress would have to do its job, too.

Anyone who voted for Donald Trump because Bernie Sanders was their first choice never listened to a word that Bernie Sanders said.

Making a false equivalency between the Republican party and the Democratic party is not only a lie, it's asinine. The Democratic party has *many* problems, but supporting American fascism is *not* one of them. Republicans would rather maintain power than save America from a madman.

Congressmen and Congresswomen need to stand up for normal Americans now, no matter if it helps or hurts their own political careers.

Mike Pence is out of the spotlight compared to Trump, but he's just as good a liar as his boss.

The State Department was granted $120 million to fight Russian meddling in our elections. It has spent $0. Why? Because Republicans control the Senate.

I am well aware that many Democratic politicians are corrupt and greedy. But compared to Ted Cruz, Mitch McConnell, Louie Gohmert, Matt Gaetz and Steve King, etc., they're unblemished saints.

When I was a kid, leg aches, bullies and homework bothered me. In college, it was boring professors, 8 a.m. classes and the Oxford comma. Now, toothaches, mosquitoes, nausea and Trump supporters are my worst enemies.

We all know that Republican congressmen and congresswomen are gutless cowards. However, they *must* please their constituents, or they are toast. Unfortunately, their constituents aren't the voters.

I know that major news channels like CNN, ABC, and others occasionally get it wrong. That's only natural -- humans make mistakes. However, if any of these stations produced fake news on purpose, they'd lose credibility with intelligent people. And that's why only Trumpsters hate them.

You. Make. No. Sense. Oh... you must be a Trump supporter!

Richard Neil Graham

Just now ·

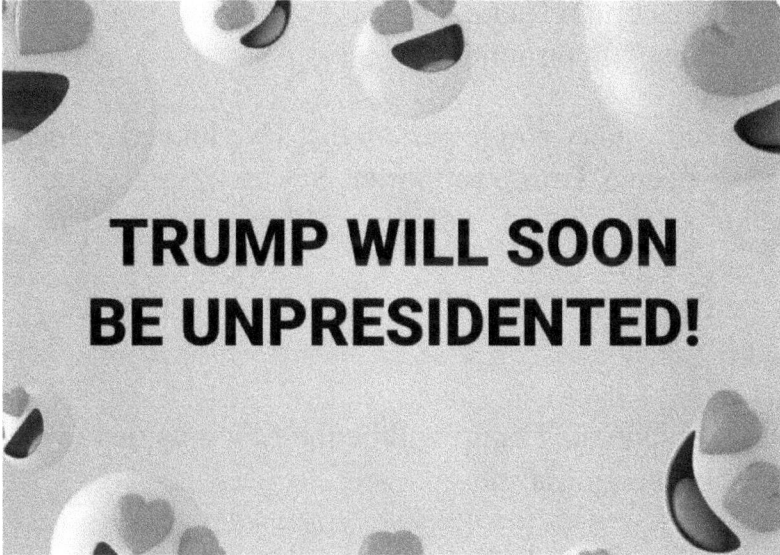

TRUMP WILL SOON BE UNPRESIDENTED!

Because Republicans are opening the economy too soon, stupid people will die. Unfortunately, they will take the innocent, unaware and intelligent down with them. Because the yahoos who lost the Civil War didn't shelter in isolation, and then spread the Coronavirus all across half the USA, we're going to have to start social distancing all over again from scratch.

Everyone in the Trump administration should be fired. By a firing squad.

Flabbergasted. adj. As if struck dumb with astonishment and surprise. - How I feel when I realize that people still support Donald Trump

How are Trump supporters like fish? They take the bait hook, line and stinker.

I have one Trumpian friend. He's as stupid as you might imagine. I keep him around for the laughs.

I just realized: Every single person that I've loaned money to is or has been a Trump supporter. Socialism under the table is apparently OK.

I miss the days when Republicans hated Russia and not America.

I predict that Donald Trump will be the first president to die on the porcelain throne.

I thought that perhaps I'd have run out of adjectives to describe Donald Trump by now. Nope. Not even close.

I was nearly attacked physically today by a Trump supporter who was so whack that he didn't even know that he was a Trump supporter. I was sad for a couple of hours afterwards. I couldn't figure out why. I should have been furious. I think it's because the gap between what I see as reality and what Trump supporters see seems an insurmountable obstacle to understanding and peace.

If you're going to vote for Trump, third party, or not at all on November 3, unfriend me now. I'm not playing.

Joe is a boating neighbor whom I'll save in a pinch, as he will me. That's separate from his political views. However, if he's drowning, I might have to consider his politics for a second before I throw the rope, ya know. It's human nature.

Let's see... we have a Republican Senate and a Republican president and a Republican Supreme Court... so why is America so fucked up? Hmmm...

Lunatic fringe. Christian evangelicals. Ammosexuals. Donald Trump. But I repeat myself.

Many women who support Trump are pretty. Pretty vacant.

Marie Antoinette supposedly said to the Parisians who were begging for bread before the French Revolution: Let them eat cake. To Republican senators like Susan Collins, who are now concerned about losing their cushy status because of the nightmare of Trump, I say, Let them eat crap!

Maybe Trump and the Evangelicals would take Covid-19 seriously if only fetuses caught the disease.

Mike Pence is either brave and stupid for not wearing a mask to the Mayo Clinic, but he's definitely an asshole.

Most Democratic politicians don't have the killer instinct necessary to play Newt Gingrich's game of divide and conquer because they care about people besides themselves.

Most Trump supporters are either poor people wishing that they were rich, or rich people terrified of becoming poor.

Trump supporters' new slogan: Live Free and Die!

Obamagate: A fake conspiracy theory created by Donald Trump meant to fire up his base of dopey dotard ammosexual hatriots.

Obamagate? Want to know what that means? I'll tell you. It's simply projection. What's projection? "Psychological projection is a defense mechanism people subconsciously employ in order to cope with difficult feelings or emotions. Psychological projection involves projecting undesirable feelings or emotions onto someone else, rather than admitting to or dealing with the unwanted feelings." - Everyday Health.com

Occasionally, someone will say something really stupid on Facebook, and I'll look at their profile to see if my perceptions are accurate. Typically, they're a Trump supporter, and I am pleased with my discernment.

Of course it's unfair to call it the #TrumpVirus and the #TrumpCrash. The virus and the crash had nothing to do with creating Trump.

OMG! I just realized that I've survived every bully in my life except Donald Trump!

Republicans voted for this Trumpian nightmare. Let *them* reap the whirlwind.

Remember the jerks who volunteered for hall monitor duties in elementary school? Those are the guys who became cops or other psychopaths in positions of power... like Putin, Kim, Trump, Duerte, Bolinsaro...

Sadly, many people who play hockey are Trump fans. I'm thinking that they may have taken too many pucks to the noggin.

Only 50 percent of Trump supporters are idiots. The other 50 percent are fucking idiots.

Pence is probably counting on his religious beliefs to keep him safe from the Coronavirus. But if he acquires the disease, he'll suddenly be praying for ventilators and quality doctors and nurses. That's how religious hypocrisy works.

Profiteers are rife during pandemics, which arrive regularly. How about a regular punishment: Exile to the country where the pandemic began?

Q-anon followers are escapees from the Trump Asylum for the Criminally Insane.

Quick integrity test: If you work in the Trump administration, you don't have any.

Reason and logic will return. America will survive. Or, evangelical Christians were right and we're all gonna die. I'm OK with that. I just don't want to be in their Heaven.

Relying on YouTube for political argument is like relying on Roseanne Barr for advice on sleeping pills.

The Trump administration is expert in four unique areas: Fake news, alternative facts, disinformation and mal-information.

Steve Mnuchin? Never trust a man with ugly glasses.

Trump supporter = The kind of person who posts something so ridiculous that you have to look at their Facebook profile to see if they're really that stupid, hoping that they were just joking.

Trump supporters are protesting self-isolation orders and gathering in large groups. Avoid Trump supporters at all costs.

Trump supporters are so stupid that they bring down America's national IQ.

Trump supporters have been calling me a libtard since 2016. Dunno what libtard means, but I'm sure am glad I've been practicing at the Libtard Shootin' Range for the last four years.

Trump supporters will go to their graves 100 percent sure of themselves... and 100 percent wrong. Sad. Bigly. Trump tells the jokes. I just write them down.

Voter suppression is the GOP's game. They use the fake threat of voter fraud to cover their tracks.

Each time I post against Donald Trump, I subconsciously grieve for friends I've lost. Not because they were right to support Trump, but because we'll each die knowing that Trump - and their acceptance of him - caused of the wreckage of our decades-old friendships.

"Sure, kids are being caged, raped and sold into human slavery, but have you see the stock market?!" - Trumpian logic

It's not the owning of guns that's the problem. Of course liberals own guns. But only people with tiny penises need AK47s and AR15s.

I love Charlie Daniels' songs. However, his politics suck like Mike Pence.

Trumpian logic: "I'm going to throw out a bullshit accusation, and it's your job to disprove it!"

Anyone claiming any kind of equivalency between Trump and the Clinton and Obama administrations is truly on hallucinogens.

MAGA. Make America Gag Again.

People carrying weapons into restaurants and supermarkets aren't thinking, "I'm prepared for an insane person to attack this restaurant." They're thinking, "I'm so scared of everything that I'm going to carry weapons into this restaurant to make normal people even more frightened than me!"

If you consider yourself "in the middle" between Trump and his opponents, you're not in the middle. You're a Trumpian. There is no middle ground between the future of America and its demise. Choose the right side.

"The tolerant left"? A canard created by fascists who can dish it out but not take it.

How many light bulbs does it take to make a Trump supporter? One. Trump supporters are not very bright.

I love almost every form of music except weepy country, overly repetitive rap, slow polka, fast classical, and "music" made by Trump-supporting musicians of all genres.

I like to argue with certain Trumpsters, but they have to have the semblance of a brain. As a result, there is only a tiny pool to choose from.

Ah! I see that you use Redneck Spellcheck!

Facebook now gives the option of seeing posts that are "Most Relevant," "Newest," or "All Comments." It's awesome, because if you select "Most Relevant," you don't see any Trumpian posts!

It's rare to find a Trump supporter with a valid argument. Cherish those moments.

Whataboutism. It's all Trump supporters know.

Old men complaining about Greta Thunberg will never get the chance to talk to world leaders, so their opinions are about as valuable as a cyst on Rush Limbaugh's ass.

I sat next to a Trump voter and his seemingly underage "wife" for about an hour tonight. He never shut up. How do I know he was a Trump supporter? I showed his wife my first three joke books and mentioned that I also had an anti-Trump book. She said, "Don't show it to him."

Donald Trump has found his new Roy Cohn. His name is Bill Barr.

There is no middle ground now. You're for America and against Trump, or you're a Republican.

American politicians who didn't vote for Donald Trump's impeachment care for their cake jobs more than they care about America.

Devin Nunes sues cows and says Democrats want to see nude pics of Donald Trump. Nunes is the ranking Republican on the House *Intelligence* Committee...

Devin Nunes says Democrats want to see nude pictures of Trump. Anyone else think of the word *projection*?

New job opportunities for Trumpsters with strong backs and weak minds: Manually operating storm drains in Trump's wall!

Lady Trumpsters made me finally understand makeup.

Donald Trump is the biggest wuss alive. He whines and cries like a little bitch. Why don't Trumpsters ever get tired of it?

We could learn from history, but, unfortunately, images speak louder than words, propaganda is stronger than common sense, and idiocy is apparently more attractive than intelligence.

There's a new reality TV show coming soon, starring Kid Rock, Ted Nugent, Kim Kardashian and Mike Love. It's called Celebrity White Whores.

I feel sad sometimes for no apparent reason. I wonder how often it's because a fascist has taken over our government.

If, as many fear, Trump's supporters act violently upon his election loss, we will finally learn where the majority of our police and National Guard stand.

I know that Stephen Miller is hard to look at. But think how fun it will be to see him when he's wearing stripes in the Federal Pen!

When I think of most Republican congressmen, "traitor" is the word that comes to mind.

Democrats will work hard for eight years to undo as much damage as possible, and then a Republican administration will come in and destroy things all over again. It's what they *do*.

The only thing more annoying than a Trumpster is a Libertarian.

U.S. military: Your duty is to the Constitution, not the president. Police: Your duty is to your city's citizens, not the president. National Guard: Your duty is to America, not the president. Congress, your duty is to protect American citizens against fascism, not lead them into it. I'm talking to you, #MoscowMitch McConnell.

Republicans have surfed on the Trump wave for as long as they could. Now they're peeling off, one by one, abandoning Trump in hopes of avoiding the rocks that Trump is speeding toward.

William Barr = Fat Hitler

Ivanka is a skank-a.

It's almost time for Fox News' annual War Against Christmas shtick.

Gutless Republicans could have shut down Trump four years ago.

Trump should have been done after he stalked Clinton from behind in the 2016 debates.

Why are Republicans defending Trump to the last man? Because they're worried about getting kicked off the gravy train.

How many of your friends have apologized for voting for Trump? Mine? *One*! Winning!

One thing about Lindsey Graham. He's quite ass toot.

Clarence Thomas has been carried by the conservative Supreme Court justices because of political correctness and his uncanny ability to take the fascist side of every argument.

> **Want to defeat Trump in 2020? Let no one dissuade you. Winners fight until the final horn. Only wimps & Russians want you to quit.**

If a warmonger like John Bolton helped to bring down Trump, it would be wonderful, but it wouldn't absolve him of his criminal cheerleading for the Iraq War.

Mike Pence says that he won't accept Turkish attacks in Syria. Neither will his husband.

Trump supporters? Idiocy is indefensible.

I sometimes laugh at Trump supporters who bought guns when Obama was in office, not realizing that liberals bought guns way before that... and then upgraded them.

I recently had my first three-day Facebook ban for mocking a Trump supporter. Relative to my previous 30-day Facebook bans, it was like a get-out-of-jail-free card!

Conservatives *hate* Hollywood movies because they're inaccurate and made by liberals. Fine. No argument from me. All I'll say is: Make a movie. What's stopping you? Besides money, intelligence, creativity, friends, inspiration, education, cooperation and historical knowledge?

Pence? That name sounds familiar? Oh, yeah... that's the last name of America's first female Vice President!

Fox News has finally convinced me that being against Donald Trump is wrong. From now on, I'm going to be *for* Trump's impeachment, *for* his conviction, and *for* his lifetime incarceration in a federal penitentiary.

Life will be even more interesting when Kanye West becomes president. At least it will kill "The Kardashians" like it killed "The Apprentice."

Great American Mysteries: Why haven't George and Kellyanne Conway divorced yet?

I trust Bill Barr as far as Kellyanne Conway can throw him.

A majority of America's senators have sold us out to Russia.

Mike Pence sure is conveniently "unaware" of a lot of things!

"I fell in love with Donald's amazing mind." - Melania Trump. "Mind" in Slovenian means "cash money." - Me

Trump staffers resist subpoenas, holding out to avoid admitting guilt. When the floodgates open, it will be glorious!

Going along with fascism to get along gives you Hitler.

People who scam millionaires go to jail. People who scam the middle class and poor get cushy jobs in the Trump administration.

The Trump administration: Only yes men and women need apply.

Hypocritical Republicans. Oops, I repeat myself.

Mass hysteria: People voting for Trump in 2016. Massive insanity: voting for Trump in 2010.

William Barr undermines America and will go down in history as the Benedict Arnold to Trump's Howdy Doody.

"Twitter Users Wonder Why Devin Nunes Keeps Bringing Up Rumored Trump Nude Photos." - Huffpost. "Easy. Because Nunes wants to see them." - Me

Sean Hannity is still crying because Marie Yovanovitch didn't.

The New York Post is Fox News-Lite.

Mike Pompeo will be so tarnished by his time with Trump that only one job option will remain: Fox News pundit.

Devin Nunes and Jim Jordan are the women that my mom warned me about.

> **For decades, Republicans & Democrats both saw Russia as an enemy. Then Putin discovered that Republicans have a price.**

Wolf Blitzer is as an inaccurate nickname as Truthful Trump.

Republicans are better at semantics and euphemisms, that's why their bullshit smells *so* good to morons.

When is the last time Republicans told the truth? When they were candidates running against Trump.

American voters not only have to defeat Trump, but they have to defeat Republican gerrymandering, election fraud, election suppression, Fox News propaganda, Russian meddling and a hostile Senate. It *won't* be easy, but dammit, we have right on our side!

Hell is: Ted Nugent covering Kid Rock's "Cowboy," sponsored by the NRA and sung by Kanye West with the Dancing Kardashians.

I believe that there are many Trump voters who will only wake up when a relative or longtime friend has been jailed or deported. By then it will be too late.

Sometimes, Trump supporters ask me why I'm so mean. I ask them why they're so stupid.

Republicans are pathetic. They once called French fries "freedom fries." They're 6th-grade bullies who never grew up.

Trump supporters feel that they finally have someone to justify their hatred, racism and bigotry... and they do.

I actually appreciate Starbucks "War on Christmas." It keeps the numbers of Trump fans in the place down.

To those investigators pursuing Devin Nunes... it's a moooolicious prosecution!

Matt Gaetz is at best a used-car salesman. How did he become a U.S. Congressman? Oh. Florida. Gotcha.

Listening to Lindsey Graham list all of the disgusting things about Trump to defend him is hilarious!

My name is Lindsey. That's why I'm outraged daily.

If you dismiss Russian interference on our elections, you're either Putin, a Putin apologist, or a Republican.

I love how Republicans attack American citizens for being disgusted by Trump, but do not attack Trump's disgusting behavior.

Like irony? How about Donald J. Trump Jr. killing a sheep?

If Republicans didn't like rubles, we'd have a conviction.

A fascist musician? Isn't that a contradiction in terms?

The prototypical Trumper wears U.S. flag shirts, promotes the U.S. Constitution, and then worships a man who shits on both.

Stephen Miller says that Democrats' attacks on him are the result of anti-Semitism. Me? I'll cop to a deep hatred of fascism enablers.

If anyone can stop Trump, it certainly won't be Republicans. They're proven traitors.

Be supremely polite to Trump supporters and change their minds with simple logic. MWAHAHAHA!!

Honest Republicans are like Jackalopes. They're extremely hard to find!

Domestic terrorists and fanatical Trump supporters overestimate themselves and underestimate us.

TRUMP'S HUGE CROWDS IN FLORIDA

RIVALED THOSE AT HIS INAUGURATION

We had checks and balances in place to stop a disaster like Trump, but #MoscowMitch McConnell and the Russians... er, Republicans, hamstrung them.

Trump is insane and no one in power near him has the guts to stop him.

What's really funny to me is that anyone still believes a single thing that Trump says.

Trump was sent by Satan to give morons jobs.

Euphoric Depression: Reconnecting with old friends on Facebook and then learning that they're Trump supporters.

If conservatives stopped complaining about the "treatment" of Trump and helped American citizens instead, America truly could be great.

I trust John Bolton and Tucker Carlson as far as I can throw Donald Trump.

Lindsey Graham says that Iran's missile attack last night is an act of war. Dude's still overcompensating for his first name.

Mike Lee of Utah gave his testicles back to Trump just one day after miraculously finding them.

If Republican politicians cared about the future of America as much as they care about the rubles in their bank accounts, Trump would never have made it this far.

Justice doesn't currently exist for Trump and his enablers. Let us have karma, at least.

Trump backtracks everything, but his cult only remembers the initial lie... and swallows that.

My theory about whether Trump supporters know about his absolute unfitness for office or not: They know, and they bury that knowledge deep inside and their unconscious inner guilt then transforms into hatred and projection against others.

One thing I really like about Trump supporters is that many use American flags instead of their ugly faces for their profile pics.

How do I know that Trump's a criminal? His biggest defenders are criminals.

I support our troops and our veterans. Why do Trump supporters ignore the Trump policies that harm veterans and their families?

Idiocy is OK. Idiocy on behalf of fascism is not.

Does Trump have kompromat on *every* Republican?!

Where do Republican politicians exchange their rubles for dollars? Enquiring minds would like to know.

If Jeffrey Epstein hadn't "committed suicide" in prison, I wonder if Lev Parnass would have spilled the beans so easily.

Some words you can make out of Ted Cruz: Curt crude rude red turd.

Lindsey Graham? Marginal ashamed airhead maligner mishandler analyser garishly greasily smearing inhaler.

Rand Paul? Darn anal nard NRA pud.

Mario Rubio? Broom burro boor boa bum rub mob.

Mitch McConnell? Lenin commie clench chemo cocci letch mice mite mole tic.

What if Donald Trump was tarred and feathered and run out of America on a rail?

It is what it is.

If I was Jewish, I'd be embarrassed to be Jared Kushner or Stephen Miller. Apparently, they're fine with just about anything if it makes money and screws people of color.

Take a look at the Facebook profile pages of some of the pro-Trump people: Many post 90 percent fake news, with 10 percent being other bullshit.

I'd be honored if my Facebook posts were being censored by red-blooded American with advanced degrees in languages. Unfortunately, I'm being outed by Trump fans who can't spell and being banned by Facebook's minimum wage censors in Bangladesh.

When I consider Donald Trump, Jeffrey Epstein and Alan Dershowitz, I think of a certain anagram of Lev Parnas: Anal Pervs.

Being a Trump supporter means that spelling is optional.

Republican senators are the most obvious hypocrites since evangelical preachers.

Congress members are voted in to look out for their constituents' interests. And they're doing a very good job of it. Unfortunately, we're not their constituents.

Do mobsters look at the Trump organization for pointers?

Republicans are great at changing the meaning of words to their own nefarious purposes. "Entitlements" for our hard-earned Social Security benefits? Fuck you!

"Collateral damage" is another Republican euphemism. It means civilian deaths during wartime.

Question: Do Trump supporters know that they're posting lies online and do it anyway - which makes them conscious purveyors of fake news - or are they really just that stupid?

I have a new word for bullshit that won't anger people who dislike profanity: "Republican!"

The Senate will vote 53-47 to acquit Trump, no matter what. 52-47 if Trump shoots Matt Gaetz on 5th Avenue.

When gambling, bet on red. Republican senators do.

Rubles speak to Republicans louder than words.

When Mike Pompeo attacked an NPR reporter and demanded that she point out the Ukraine on a map of the world, he was projecting... he knew that Trump couldn't pick out the USA on a map, let alone the Ukraine.

Conservatism means yesterday. How can you move forward when you are always looking backward?

I saw some dude spouting idiotic conspiracy theories on Twitter. I said, "QANON? Really? LMFAO. Hey, Lindsey Graham is making gay pizza for captured Republican children in the White House basement! Go in guns-a-blazing and save them!"

I wouldn't buy John Bolton's book if it came with a free mustache-care treatment package.

Mitt Romney was correct when he said that 47 percent of Americans do not pay taxes. That's because they're too poor, or so wealthy that they can afford lawyers to find the loopholes. America survives on *our* middle-class backs, my friends.

Several Republican senators broke the rules of the Senate impeachment trial by stepping out of the chamber to give an interviews or otherwise fuck off. Funny how they're so adamant about the rules when they apply to their colleagues across the aisle.

We're headed for a violent revolution, thanks to American politicians who sold their souls for Russian rubles. Rebuttals?

Republicans may have broken my heart, but they have steeled my spine.

Want a job in the Trump administration? Urine!

Trump, Pence, Dershowitz, Epstein, Barr, Pompeo and Mulvaney are all Humbert Humbert, but without any literary value.

I started a cool Facebook group to oppose Trump called Nasty Women & Bad Hombres. It's been an awesome experience, and I've met hundres of *true* American patriots.

Trump supporters mock liberals as wanting free stuff from the government. And they have a point. I want air and water free of pollution, government free of corruption, and the American president free from Russian influence.

Let's say that you're a moron. And let's say that you're a Trump supporter. Oh, but I repeat myself.

When the Trump pee tape is finally released, Republicans will say that Trump was just providing a free hot shower to poverty-stricken Russian women.

Rush Limbaugh is a big fat piece of shit. So is Newt Gingrich. If you don't think that language matters, look up Newt Gingrich. If you think politics is a gentleman's game that must be played fairly, read up on Lee Atwater and Karl Rove. Politics is about gaining and keeping power. That's it.

Republicans have put Mentos in America's bottle of Coke and screwed the top on tight. Hang on. Something is going to explode.

Trying to choose the dumbest Republican congressman is very difficult.

Trying to pick the most racist Republican congressman is very difficult.

Trying to pick the most idiotic Republican congressman is extremely difficult.

Trying to find an honest Republican congressman is just about impossible.

If you like Trump, you're dirty. If Trump likes you, you're dirty.

If you like Trump, you're like Mike Pence. A sycophant.

Donald Trump did one wonderful thing for me. He completely cleaned up my Facebook friends list.

Things that Trigger Trump Supporters, Edition #1

Science. - Wayne Jones
Disrespect of our fearless and all-powerful leader! - Bill Romero
Obama. - Mario Tellez
And Hillary. - Dana Ferraro
Powerful women. - Lauri Paulsen
Anything I say. - Robert Broido
Cheetos. Kyle Chamblin
Gun safety.
AOC. Al Merrick
Truth. - Derrick Suggs

Things that Trigger Trump Supporters, Edition #2

A black hand touching them. - Derek Guth
Jesus' actual teachings. - Andrea Martin
Planned Parenthood. - Deidre Christensen
Free and fair elections. - Ubahn Xomar Jarah
Asked to recite Bible verses. - Ubahn Xomar Jarah
Words with three syllables. - Pete Roberts
Tax returns. - Angela Ochoa
Mushroom jokes. - Dan Bowman
Simple. 'Fuck Trump.'
Gay people.

Things that Trigger Trump Supporters, Edition #3

Human rights.
Mexicans.
Black people.
People of color.
Intelligence.
8th grade.
A non-Trump supporter. - Lauri Paulsen
Night.
Skittles.

Things that Trigger Trump Supporters, Edition #4

Hoodies.
Books.
Reading.
Learning.
Power outages during Fox News broadcasts.
Children who aren't white.
Drug tests.
Psychiatrists.
Elections."- Lauri Paulsen

Things that Trigger Trump Supporters, Edition #5

Winning. - Lauri Paulsen
Teeth.
Meth.
Opiods.
Liberals.
College.
Advanced degrees.
States they've never visited.
Countries they've heard of.
Women with brains.

Things that Trigger Trump Supporters, Edition #6

Strong women.
Democrats.
Dentists.
Barbers.
Thought.
Mark Twain.
Books.
Libraries.
Sex.
Opinions.

Things that Trigger Trump Supporters, Edition #7

Drinks without straws.
Blue states.
Alcohol on Sundays.
Words they don't understand.
Dictionaries.
Puns.
Logic.
Environmentalism.
People looking for a better life.
Soccer.

Things that Trigger Trump Supporters, Edition #8

Birth control.
Bare arms on presidents' wives who ain't white.
Clean bathrooms.
People with IQs over 100. - Tom Pavlock
Unshared friends' sisters.
Real tans.
Scientific consensus. - Deidre Christensen

4: Say What?

"Some things you must always be unable to bear. Some things you must never stop refusing to bear. Injustice and outrage and dishonor and shame. No matter how young you are or how old you have got. Not for kudos and not for cash: your picture in the paper nor money in the bank either. Just refuse to bear them." - William Faulkner, Intruder in the Dust

"Moral compass?" I don't think that those words mean what you think they mean, Ivanka.

"Another way of calling Trump what he is, but not getting banned on Facebook: basura gringo!" - Shonny Bonn

"Trump is blanca refuse." - Laura Carver Sevy

"Donald Trump and Boris Johnson can make a $5,000 suit look like it came from the Goodwill." - Kathy Kendrick

"It should be obvious but a large segment of the mostly conservative American people actually fall for this counterfeit tough-guy schtick." - Scot Gassen. "Even when they run from the scene after a pickup truck backfires..." - Me

"I'll bring the hookers!" - Donald Trump

"Indicted' means free to go, right?" - Donald Trump

"Stupid people love fascism. It eliminates the requirement of thinking." - Nicholas Luis Sevilla

"A recent survey found that 48 percent approve of the job Trump is doing." - Christian Broadcasting News. 48 percent of Americans approve of eating themselves to death." - Me.

"America is the home of the hypocrite." - The Violent Femmes

"He is a Picasso of pettiness; a Shakespeare of shit... He makes Nixon look trustworthy and George W look smart... If being a twat was a TV show, Trump would be the boxed set." - British writer Nate White

"In fairness to Laura Ingraham, every time she talks she disproves white supremacy." - Andy Borowitz

"It's not a tornado. It's a freedom wind." - Kn Lam

"President Trump is 'absolutely, deadly serious' about imposing a 5 percent tariff on Mexican goods next week." - Mick Mulvaney, acting White House chief of staff. "Well, he may or not be serious, but he's absolutely deadly." - Me

"Right-wing strict conservative Christian element, big business having their dirty fucking hands in all the politics, Rupert Murdoch is a fucking menace in and of himself, cunts like Barnaby Joyce are selling off our water to corporations while our farmers are paying $650/mega litre to keep livestock alive and being scammed out of hay, Liberal Party (name is ironic they're our Republicans) & Coalition cutting our National Disability Insurance Scheme funding by over a billion dollars to present a 'budget surplus,' trying to cut Medicare, social security funding, cutting penalty rates for workers, the list goes on. We're in crisis and half the country is too self absorbed to have realized it." - Australia's Aleisha Lucas. "Sounds like the identical problem with the USA, but with a different accent." - Me

"Trump is a sexual predator, criminal, sociopath, malignant narcissist and whimshit." - Alan Litsey

"Trump now says he only wants Trump supporters at his 4th of July celebration in Washington, D.C. to honor him only." - Michael Malek. "All 3?" - Me

"Send the Native Amazonians more rakes, immediately!" - Donald Trump

Regarding the current presidency: "You can respect your home, but not the termites infesting it." - Nancy Frederick Sussan

"If you deride the fool, I like it." - My 84-year-old boating neighbor, Commodore Ed, after I gave him a copy of my book, Trumpsters & Traitors

"It's all well and good, 2nd amendment haters, but you're going to have to pry my penis extender from my cold, dead hands." - Joe Ammosexual

"This, too, shall pass." - Me. "Like a kidney stone. Painful in the passing." - Sharon Meyers

"Mitt Romney actually read the memo & knows Trump's days are numbered. Good for him for calling the situation deeply troubling!" - Some lady on Facebook. "He'll exonerate Trump tomorrow for a free cookie." - Me

"The closest thing... even more than the Watergate hearings... to the current strain on my brain was the daily Vietnam body count being broadcast on the nightly news..." Richard Leighton

Chateaubriand (counter-revolutionary French thinker) once said: 'You have to keep the population uneducated and well fed. Uneducated to be able to lie to them, well fed to cut their will to act.' - Arnaud Selukov

"It's not the America I signed up for." - Richard, an immigrant friend from Switzerland

What does Trump's existence prove? That big mouths are an evolutionary advantage?

"I would pay a couple of my paychecks to see the meltdown that would occur if Bill Barr recused himself from Trump's Ukraine fiasco." - Derrick S. Suggs

"If saying the whistleblower should be executed isn't witness intimidation and witness tampering, then a whole lot of mafia guys need to be released." - Mike Desposito

"You can't fire me. I quit! You can't quit. You're fired!" - The most frequent quotes overheard in the Oval Office.

When Donald Trump says he's working hard, I hear "hardly working."

When Donald Trump says "many people say," I hear "I just made that up."

When Donald Trump says "Hillary Clinton," I hear, "I don't want to go to prison!"

When Donald Trump says "Barack Obama," I hear "I can't even compete."

When Donald Trump says "Covfefe," I hear, "padded cell available."

"In my great and unmatched wisdom, I will totally destroy and obliterate America to accumulate as much money as possible for myself and Ivanka, and we will live together forever in a golden tower in Moscow." - Donald Trump, 10-7-2019

"Giuliani's new 20-year-old spokeswoman has a shady resume and links to Ukraine henchmen." - Politico. Allen told Politico that she got the job after tackling "incredibly challenging questions" during multiple interviews with Giuliani and his staff. Some of the questions included: "Will you take your clothes off for money?" "What is your bust size?" "Do you know what a honey trap is?"

"Velcom to ze new Amerika, comrades. Be vorst." - Melania

"Trump's nuclear button isn't bigger than Kim's. Trump's hands are smaller." - Dave Davidson

"Sick and ignorant people are easily controlled. Good healthcare and good education are freedom. Vote freedom." - Rich Kaelin

"Chloroquine is to Kool-Aid as Donald Trump is to Jim Jones." - Michael Thomas Daniel

"I must admit that my understanding of the cosmos ends at my knowledge of Uranus." - Mike Pence to Donald Trump

"I think that everything Donald Trump says is to cover his ass." - Me. - "That's why it takes him so long to say it." - Rose Romero

"If you could sacrifice one person to end COVID-19, who would it be and why Trump?" - Joanne Evony

"I'm going to the gun show." - Trumpian ammosexual. "Don't you mean the small penis convention?" - Me

"Some lady Trumpster was harassing me on Facebook, so I told her to go home and brush her *tooth*. I got 30 days in Facebook Jail." - Artie Giordano

"Trump donates salary for last quarter of 2019 for seventh time." - Me

"Trump's like both ventriloquist and the dummy because he talks out of his mouth and his ass at the same time." - Anthony Stevem

"What do you expect from a guy who received five deferments from Vietnam and wears more make-up than Tammy Faye Bakker?" - Jonathan Cain

Need Democratic Slogans? I'll start:

If It Says Trump, Kick its Rump!

Take a Dump & Defeat Trump

And You Thought Hillary Was a Bitch

Trump? Fuck Off and Die

Trump Destroyed America & Putin Didn't Have to Fire a Shot

"If it sounds like Kid Rock, kick it in the c**k!" - Aaron Bjerk

"Take PAC money, don't get my vote, honey!" - Aaron Bjerk

"Don't be a country bumpkin for Vladimir Trumpkin!" - Aaron Bjerk

"Only *you* can prevent a GOP dumpster fire!" - Aaron Bjerk

"Four whores and seven indictments ago... Our orange father bestowed upon us great shame and humiliation." - Aaron Bjerk

"Any of Dem is better than him." - Derek. S. Suggs

"Don't "*Red*" on me!" - Aaron Bjerk

"We took a y*uge* 'Trump' and clogged America." - Aaron Bjerk

"Roses are red, violets are blue… Fuck Trump." - Aaron Bjerk

"I'd vote for my dog over tRump." - Kathleen Orth-Thomas

"What do you have to lose?" - Donald Trump

Except for your citizenship, savings and freedom?

Even if it ruins the businesses of American family farms...

Even if it ruins our relationships with our allies...

Even if it ruins our air and water...

Even if it ruins women's rights...

Even if it ruins the meaning of the Statue of Liberty...

Even if it ruins America's standing in the world...

Even if it ruins the rule of law...

Even if it ruins foreign travel to America...

Even if it ruins the lives of innocent children that Trump caged...
Even if it ruins our national parks...

Even if it ruins the ideal of America that so many of us used to hold on our hearts...

What else needs to be ruined before you'll finally admit that your vote for Trump helped to screw all but the wealthiest Americans, including yourselves?

"The Democrats are human scum!" - Donald Trump. Next it will be: "Independents are human scum!" Then: "Republican senators who voted against me are human scum!" Finally: "The American people are human scum!"

"I can just imagine the knuckle-dragging, slack-jawed MAGAts cheering the destruction of Persian culture sites because they care nothing for history, antiquities and culture. Ignorant morons." - Anne Hutchins. "But attack a Chik-Fil-A and it's war." - Me. "Here's a question. What do you think Trump's idea of cultural sites are?" - Don Williams. "McDonald's?" - Citizen Bumatay. "You know who else targeted cultural treasures? The *Taliban*!" - Me

"McConnell Attempts to Shield GOP From Potential Trump Fallout." - Bloomberg. "What's he gonna do, hide them under his turtle shell?" - Me

"It was a beautiful impeachment." - Dan Chusid. "With 10 times the attendees as his inauguration!" - Me

Donald Trump writing a tweet demanding that people in his administration defy Congress: "Don't respond to any Subpeena... Subpina... Suppina... Subpyna... Subina... Speena... Ah, fuck it! Any legal papperwerk from Congress!"

"Giuliani is not doing this (defending Trump) pro bono," Martin Greenspan. "I know. He's doing it pro boner." - Me

"Melania who?" - Donald Trump

> # When the "president" of the United States shouldn't be the leader of F-Troop, let alone the free world.

"I remember feeling hate and loathing for someone years ago when he came into a record shop where I worked and tried picking up some young teen and preteen girls shopping. We chased him out as he raged that he and his father would destroy us. This monster was in his mid-20s but already an obnoxious budding pedophile. Oh. Wait. It was the same person who is now our shameful, deceitful president." - James Pina

"Trump and his associates? The Indictables." - Howard Paley

"The good news for Trump is that 100 percent of evil dictators are against his impeachment." - Al Merrick

"Rudy Jailiani." - Ronald Silverman

"Arizona Governor Says Christians Shouldn't Have to Serve Gays." Wait... what Bible passage is that from? I went to church for 25 years. How did I miss Jesus saying that?" - Me

"Evangelists are Evil Angels." - Alexandria Clendenning

"Hi. I'm not available right now. If this is an emergency, please call my employer at 1-800-Vladimir." - Donald Trump's answering machine

"Alternative facts, bitches! No one second guesses Trump's mouthpiece!" - Stephen Miller

"Donald Trump is not as smart as a 5th grader." - Rob VanVoorhis. "Fifth grader? He's not even smarter than a cheese grater." - Jonathan Moorehead

"I had an epiphany this morning. 'Right to Life' is as phony as the 'Patriot Act' and 'Right to Work.' It has nothing to do with life other than the control of women." - Peggy Mackenzie. "Those are euphemisms meant to distort reality." - Me

"John Kelly Was Unequipped to Handle Trump's 'Genius.' " - The White House (not a joke)

"I'm not very political here, but you should know if you bring your vehicle to me for work and it has a Trump bumper sticker on it, I charge a hidden dumbfuck fee." - Prick Offerman on Twitter

"Trump unmasks traitors posing as lifelong patriots." - Mark Timothy Ramsey

"Something big just happened!" - Donald Trump. "You had a bowel movement?" - Me

"These are people who plot and scheme, who measure the price that others will have to pay because of their decisions. Now, a great reckoning is upon their party, with few equipped with the moral tools needed to make the choice. They *must* hang on - there really is nothing left for them - it's too late." - Joe Biuso

"Federal judge rules Trump administration must provide mental health services to migrant families separated at border." - The Hill. "Trump needs those services more." - Me

"Lest we forget, many have never faced any sort of test - these so-called intelligent, educated persons - with the majority being lawyers. Not poor people who joined the US Army to escape crushing poverty. Not workers who've made their way through life by dint of their strong backs." - Joe Biuso

"With their wagons hitched to a runaway wild horse, not yet broken by the reality of DC politics, their choice is clear. Forsake Trump and risk being primaried out. Or, hang on for dear life as the wagon heads pell mell toward that cliff. Little, really, for them to choose from." - Joe Biuso

"Once Trump became the titular head of the Republican party, without knowledge of the party's history, or for that matter, any history, the Republican leadership was compelled by the populist nature of Trump's election to get into line behind their leader." - Joe Biuso

"The Republican party dies, or America does." - Me

Defense attorney for Trump: "Your Honor, my client is too stupid to know that he committed a crime." Judge: "Counsel, I agree. He can go on being president."

"Scottish Government Says Trump Org Refuses to Pay Legal Bills After Losing Wind Farm Lawsuit." - Law & Crime headline. "Hold Hole #18 for Ransom." - Me

"South Carolina group can reject gays and Jews as foster parents, Trump admin says." - Newspaper headline. "It's only fair. South Carolinians are already banned from being intelligent." - Me

"Success is an ugly thing. Men are deceived by its false resemblances to merit.... They confound the brilliance of the firmament with the star-shaped footprints of a duck in the mud." - Victor Hugo, Les Misérables

"Am I being audited because I'm a Christian?" - Donald Trump. "I don't know. Do I have to pay taxes because you don't?" - Me

"58.3 million 'followers' on Twitter, Trump? Hah! Look at that list. I'll bet that 58.2 million are here just like me, anxiously awaiting your final tweet: 'Help! I've been arrested for treason and I nee...'" - Me

"Republicans are attacking Michael Cohen, not defending Donald Trump. A reminder: those attacking Cohen believed him the first time, when he was lying." - Andrew Spiciarich

"The Devil wanted Donald Trump as president." - God

> ## Trump's bringing strangers together, strengthening our bonds, steeling our souls, lighting our torches, stoking our anger.

"If someone jumps out of a building on the 30th floor and is still alive when they pass the 20th floor, they might think they are winning, but the ground floor will have the last word on that subject." - Devan Hermanson on Twitter

"We can take phones away from 7-year-olds when they order pizza, so why can't we take the phone away from our president? - Jason Johnson, Political Editor, TheRoot.com

"Vice: a very good, maddening, motivating movie about a very evil man, his evil wife, and the absolute evil of absolute power. Never forget... impeach and resist." – Darrin Mortensen

"I'm gonna smack an active hornets' nest with a big stick, and I'm going to do it with an audience of my supporters' naked babies. It's the only way that they can prove their love for me. Besides giving me cash." - Donald Trump

"My war-like rhetoric has made America safer and lowered our citizens' anxiety levels. Bigly." - Donald Trump

"Yes, we have a bumpy road ahead. We took back the House in 2018, and then the Senate and the presidency in 2020. State houses as well. Then we start fixing the systemic problems that allowed someone like Trump to get elected." - Mike Boos

"Trump's lawyer is convicted of making payments to a porn star and a Playboy playmate to silence them about their affairs with Trump, but the stupid son of a bitch denies that these affairs happened. If no affairs took place, why were payments made? Of course, his ignorant and stupid American supporters will believe his bullshit denial." - William Shaedler

Republicanism: "Money in my pocket over my country."

"Don't look at my finances, taxes, sexual assaults or charities. Look at what's important. Squirrel!" - Donald Trump

"We don't have any money for Nebraska and Iowa losers who chose to live in a flood plain and are going broke because of the government's trade wars and tariffs!" - Donald Trump

"We seek an approach to refugee resettlement that is designed to help these horribly treated people by abandoning them to their fate in their home countries." - Donald Trump

"No nation on Earth has an interest in seeing this band of criminals arm itself with nuclear weapons and missiles. But as long as I'm president, that's what we're going to do. Believe me." - Donald Trump

"The United States is one out of 193 countries in the United Nations, and yet we pay 22 percent of the entire budget. That's like nine tenths. Very, very expensive. Bigly expensive." - Donald Trump

Trump voter: "St. Peter, I wanted to watch the game and not to have to think about marginalized Americans abused horribly by the police. I never thought about them during the week, either, but asking me to do it on one of the four days of NFL games each week was like slavery." St. Peter: "Go to Hell."

"It is a massive source of embarrassment to the United Nations that some governments with egregious human rights records sit on the UN Human Rights Council. My administration, for example." - Donald Trump

"The Democratic memo was too long. I fell asleep before I got to the part about me selling out America to Russia." - Donald Trump

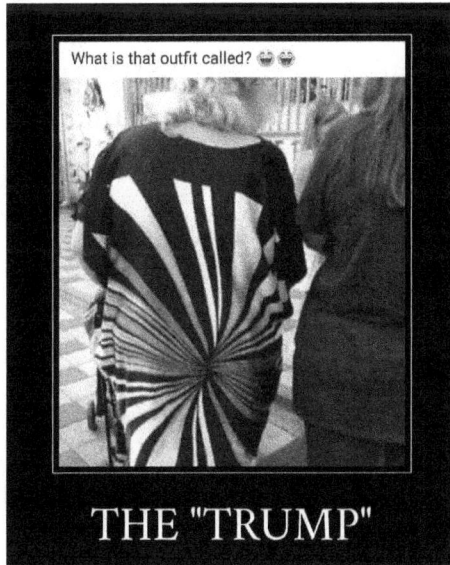

What is that outfit called? 😵 😵

THE "TRUMP"

"What would it take for you to believe in God? What would it take for you to not believe in God?" - Andrew Smith. "There is no demonstrative evidence of any deity." - Steven Noad. "The question being, what evidence is required? A great big foot coming down out of the sky and squishing Trump Monty-Python style?" - Andrew Smith. "That would do it for me." - Me

"I hope Vladimir Putin ends the shutdown soon." - Ronald Silverman

"Why is Bolton protecting Trump?" - Bertha Cunningham-Leake. "Bolton is protecting Bolton." - Me

"For decades, Republicans and Democrats both saw Russia as an enemy. Then Putin discovered that Republicans have a price." - Gary Gaffney

"Ivanka who?" - Donald Trump

"If I was in the military, I'd be the greatest warrior of all time, better than Tony Stark, John Carter and Jack Reacher, combined." - Donald Trump

"I imagine that Trump thinks 'exonerated' is some kind of soda pop." - Mark Toma

"It vas the vest of times, it vas the vorst of times." - Moronia Trump. "Ahhhh... the first line from the book about Donald and Melania, "A Tale of Two Shitties." - Aaron Bjerk

"My apologies to my neighbors for all of the yelling and screaming and swearing... I was channel surfing and stopped on Faux News for a couple of minutes." - Tom Tusor

"George Conway, Steve Schmidt & Rick Wilson burn Trump in op-ed." - News headline. "Average Americans have been doing it free for four fucking years! - Me

"On this day, 2014, President Obama normalizes relations with Cuba. On this day now, Trump is blowing some Russian." - Gil Prothero

The Senate acquitted him... but he's still guilty as sin.

"My grandchildren and their children will be taught that DJT was impeached. He will *forever* wear the scarlet letter I." - Maria Shafer

"I used to be such a sweet, sweet thing, till they got a hold of me." - Alice Cooper. "Me too, till Trump the Chump." - Me

EVIL TWIRP

"Facebook jailings are completely capricious, arbitrary and random... I got jailed for comparing Miller to Goebbels." - Jeff Cooper

"Trump is the dumbest son of a bitch on Earth. That's a planet, you know." - Kathy Gail

"I like presidents who aren't Russian assets." - Virginia Shaddock MacGregor. "Or American asses." - Me

"Evangenitals." - John P. Holloway

"So, things escalated initially, according to Trump because Iran killed an American contractor? I don't remember things escalating when N. Korea killed Otto Warmbier. I don't remember things escalating when Saudi Arabia killed Jamal Khashoggi. I don't remember things escalating when a Saudi killed three servicemen on a military base in Florida recently." - Ted DeBont

"Let's Play War. With Your Kids. Trump 2020." - Gary Gaffney

"What Trump empire?" - Tom Tusor. "Shit buildings built on near slave labor for Saudis, Russians and Mafiosi." - Me

"Q: What's the difference between Donald Trump and Ronald Reagan? A: If Trump gets Alzheimer's, his IQ will go up." - Shiro Ken

"In 2013, psychiatrists Dr. Samuel Leistedt and Dr. Paul Linkowski published a study of the portrayal of psychopaths in film, and cited the Gekko character as a realistic portrayal of the successful, 'corporate psychopath': 'In terms of a 'successful psychopath,' they write, 'Gordon Gekko from Wall Street (1987) is probably one of the most interesting, manipulative, psychopathic fictional characters to date." - Wikipedia. "Unfortunately, Donald J. Trump is not fiction." - Me

"I came. I saw. I lied." - Donald Trump

"He can be manipulated psychologically." - George Butel on Trump. "Isn't a brain required for that?" - Me

"President Crybaby has to be the creepiest weirdo to ever be slimed into the White House. Just his bizarre appearance of a chem-tanned orange face with purpleish bags under his empty, soulless eyes; rat's nest pompadour coif; an exaggerated red neck tie as a phallic substitute; laughable ill-fitting clown suit; slurred, often unintelligible speech, and swaggering bullies gait; should be a tip off that this humanoid ain't right in the head." - Scot Gassen

"We don't pay taxes; only the little people pay taxes." - Leona Helmsley

"Taxes? What are taxes?" - Donald Trump

"What first comes to your mind when you hear the names Pompeo, Pence and Barr?" - Glenn Adams. "Traitors hoping to hasten the Apocalypse." - Me

"Blow jobs are illegal if you're a Democrat." - Lindsey Graham

"I prefer criminals that don't get caught." - Donald Trump

"Trump's gotta have something on Graham, Nunes and Cruz, because he really dragged those guys through the mud and they still give him the press version of a blow job every day." - Aaron Bjerk.

"Exactly. Would *you* forgive a man like Trump dissing your wife and your father?" - Me

"Among other (Alan) Dershowitz clients: Claus von Bülow, O.J. Simpson, Mike Tyson, Jeffrey Epstein, and Harvey Weinstein. Individual #1 sounds like a perfect fit." - Scoop Cooper

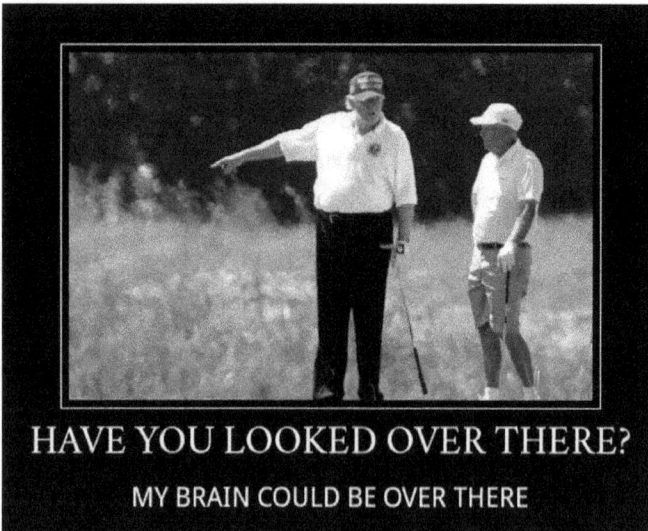

HAVE YOU LOOKED OVER THERE?

MY BRAIN COULD BE OVER THERE

"White undersupremacists." - Nicholas J. Evancik

"Trump's poll numbers have tanked in the last month — and even his supporters agree he broke the law." - CNN. "Please, continue." - Me

"Trump, Moscow Mitch and Republicans are again talking about cutting Social Security. It takes aim at Trump's strongest age group." - John Portelli. "Apparently, they're too stupid to care. Racism and owning the libs are a higher priority than money." - Me

"You're charged with stealing $1 million from a bank. How do you plead?"

"I plead the Trump Defense, your Honor."

"The Trump Defense? What's that?"

"Innocent By Alternative Facts, sir."

"That cannot be argued with. I'm going to have to let you go."

"Thank you, your Honor."

"They should take his (Trump's) threats seriously. He's nothing but a mobster, a two-bit criminal with extreme mental illness." - Gary Hanick. "I do. Ivanovich does. Parnas does. Cohen does. Epstein did." - Me

"Sadly, the vast majority of those on the right have their index fingers planted firmly in their ears... quite an accomplishment considering they have their thumbs up their asses as well." - Chris Parker

"Trump regularly can't remember what he's said or been told." - News story headline. "Me neither, but I *can* remember the nuclear codes. Oops!" - Me

"I really feel for Chump. How does such an innocent man get caught up in so much criminality against his will? What are the odds?" - Pete Roberts

"Modern thrill-seeking: Wearing a Hillary Clinton T-shirt to a Trump rally." - Me. "Or a Bernie rally." - Timothy Carlson. "What are Berners going to do? Sing Kumbaya at them loudly?" - Me

"You do not have to prove innocence in the United States." - Greg Hoover. "So, you agree: witnesses that can prove Trump's guilt should appear. I concur!" - Me

"Manage money like a millionaire." - Facebook ad. "Have your father give you $400 million, then lose $399 million of it." - Donald Trump

"We are your overlords." - Led Zeppelin, stolen by Putin, soon to be stated to America

"No Supreme Court pick so close to an election." - Mitch McConnell

Trump's next job: License Plate Maker

"No impeachment so close to an election." - Mitch McConnell. "No representation for the majority of the U.S. population." - Mitch McConnell, implied

"If a president did something that he believes will help him get elected — in the public interest — that cannot be the kind of quid pro quo that results in impeachment." - Alan Dershowitz "It's not illegal when the president does it." - Richard Nixon. "Trump is so crooked, when he dies, they'll have to screw him into the ground." - B.K. Fleming

"Serious question: If you think Jesus sent us Trump, what about Trump reminds you of Jesus?" - Matthew Grant. "He walks, he talks, and he is occasionally kind to whores?" - Me

"Congratulations to the Kansas City Chiefs. It's wonderful to have a Native American team win the Super Bowl." - Donald Trump

"Wonder how (Trump lawyer Pat) Cipollone explains his lack of ethics and lying to his 10 kids?" - Ron Massad. "None of them are *his* kids?" - Me

"Liberals who attend college are 'elitist,' but conservatives who spend $3.4 million on a Super Bowl golf party aren't?" - Bill Allyn

"O.J. Simpson was acquitted, too." - Steven Silverman

"If I could choose anyone, living or dead, to be president of the United States, who would it it be? Hmm... OK. Living: Bernie Sanders. Dead: Donald Trump." - Mohan Eappen

"Trump Officials Worry President Will Retaliate If They Report Unethical Acts." - Headline." Be a patriot, make the report, then get a better job and live with a clear conscience." - Me

But not Putin.

TRUMP HAS ATTACKED FAUCI, OBAMA
BIDEN, THE MEDIA & POLLS

"Grandpa, can you describe in three words how America was destroyed from within?" "Sure, child. 'Ownin' the libtards!' "

"Yo, Anti-Semite!" - Me, yelling at Trump

"Let's have Trump read 'Tucson' out loud." - Renee Brunette

"Democracy. It's a hoax!" - Donald Trump

"A guy walks into a Barr....and shoots him." - TJ Sears

"Right now there is a great deal of Russian bullshit flooding Facebook." - Carl Rody. "Nyet." - Me

"Biden? I was going to vote for him until I found out how sleepy he was." - Kathy Carter. "Does it matter?" - Marsha Higginbotham. "Not to me. Betcha it matters to him, though." - Me

"George Bush doesn't care about black people." - Kanye West. "And Donald Trump does?" - Me

"The problem with conspiracy theories is that when they're real you almost never know about them, and when you know about them, they're almost never real." - Rich Kaelin

"Q-Anon is the right-wing organization that thinks the Tea Party is too liberal." - Jimmy Breazeale

"The rest of the world sees the United States as a complete failure at this point. And it's all because of hyper-partisan politics." - Rich Kaelin. "Not at all. Partisan politics is merely a *symptom* of America's pathological illness of racism and greed." - Me

"He's not a typical politician." - My next door neighbor yakking about Trump, almost four years in...

"Damned white supremacists are taking over Hawaiian shirts. We must stop this. I love mine." - Kim Kermes. "I hear that! They stole our flag and tiki torches, too, the fucks." - Me

"Trumpsters have no idea what it means to be liberal. I'm tired of the snowflake reference." - Cathy Siano Battaglia. "I like to call them Trumpflakes." - Doug Tauber. "What's funny is that if you turn that label back on a Trumper, they lose their shit!" - Me. "And then, they accuse you of bullying because you resorted to name calling, being totally oblivious that they called you snowflake in the first place." - Doug Tauber. "And guess who gets Facebook jail?" - Me

"I just mailed something on Tuesday and my estimate to get to California on my tracking number is next Monday. That never happens. I usually get things delivered in two days." - A friend in Portland, Oregon. "My birthday is next May. Please mail my gifts now so that they arrive on time."

"Trump? This clown is a moron." - Salvador Robert Arce. "No! This moron is a clown!" - Me

"President Trump is claiming that Sen. Kamala Harris was his 'number-one pick' to be named presumptive Democratic nominee Joe Biden's running mate." - The Hill. "He's the #1 Prick, so he should know." - Me

"My name is Donald Trump and I am the Commander in Thief!"

"What kind of shithead president admits on television that he's sabotaging the United States' post office to stop people from voting safely by mail during a deadly pandemic?' - A recent Facebook meme. "One installed by American traitors and Russian oligarchs." - Me

"Will 'Mother' allow Pence to debate Harris?" - MSN commentator. Translation: Will Mike Pence's beard allow him in the same hall as a woman who's, *gasp*, not his wife?

My current life goal? To see Trump hoist by his own petard.

"How big a dick is Matt Gaetz?" - Marty Conmy. "A huge dick with a small one." - Me

"I find it fascinating that the same people who claim to be patriots are flying the flag of fascists, and simultaneously telling black people not to disrespect the 'American' flag by kneeling at a football game." - Philippe Esteva

"Who? Steve Bannon? Hardly knew the guy. I know he used to work here. I think I saw him around once, maybe twice. Sloppy guy. We had to get rid of him." - Jimmy Breazeale

"Someone, please, buy California some more rakes!" - Me. "Why can't you lazy Californians clean up like they do in Norway? Herr Drumpf was quite impressed with them Nordskis and how hygienic they are with forest tidiness." - Joe Biuso. "Just drop the branches and leaves off at the White House for Melania's Blair Bitch Project." - Me

"Jerry Falwell Jr. needs to resign and spend more time watching his family." - Me

"Mommy, I want to grow up to be president!" "Why, honey?" "Because you can get away with *everything*!"

"You can't say white trash on Facebook. However, pale garbage is still permitted." - Me. "As is translucent detritus.' " - James Fine

5 Pinhead Predictions

HI. I'M AN AMERICAN NAZI

TRUMP SENT ME

2020 is the last year of a decade and the year that Donald Trump gets fired from the first job he's ever had.

Once Trump forgets about Space Force, I predict that he chooses a new endeavor: Submarine Force! To explore that wet stuff off the coast of the Mar-A-Lago swamp.

After Trump, it will probably be another 75 years before we see nepotism again in a presidential administration.

When it comes down to it, the military *may* have to choose to defend the Constitution or Trump. I believe that they'll choose to defend the Constitution. *Some* of it, anyway. (Sort of positive, right?)

Sane Americans outnumber Trumpsters at least two to one, but if we don't fight back against their racism and hate, they win. We beat them in 1865 and we'll do it again.

I predict that within 10 years, immigrants seeking U.S. citizenship will be required to know the difference between Marvel and DC comic book characters. And that's it.

When Trump is finally gone, the complete truth will be realized, and those who supported him will be exposed as traitors or fools.

Michael Cohen is a thug who sold his soul for Donald Trump. If he sells out Donald Trump, he can become an American hero. Strange how life can twist and turn.

Note every single egregious legislative decision that Donald Trump makes. We'll reverse them all when Trump is in prison.

Members of the Trump administration feel bulletproof now, but that won't last forever. Just ask the French monarchy. Vote *Blue* in 2020 or it's Trump forever. Make your stand in public. Show your guts, intelligence and patriotism before Trump's environmental policies kill us all. And then stand by it, so your descendants, if they survive Trump's anti-environmental greed-mongering, will know that you were a true patriot, and not a Trumpriot.

Michelle Malkin never has to worry about being unemployed. Trump will always have a job for a maid.

I will be a much more pleasant person once Trump is finally gone.

I'm the worst prognosticator in the world, but if the worst possibility should occur and Trump escapes impeachment *and* is reelected, we can tie his hands by keeping the House and taking the Senate. I believe that momentum is on the Democratic side. It's only the future of America that is at stake, after all.

If Trump skates, America is truly finished. Get some apathetic people to vote!

I traveled east about three years ago and walked the grassy area at Kent State where people died. I am not embarrassed to say that I cried. I am not shy about saying that I fear Trump will make it happen again.

I predict that "Kamala" will soon be moving up the rankings of popular baby names.

In about 10 years, it will be difficult to find anyone who will admit to having voted for Donald Trump.

Dems can't win... until they stand up loud and clear against totalitarianism.

Remember all the crazy things that we learned about Saddam Hussein after he lost power? We're going to learn the same things about Donald Trump. Keep yourself alive; it will be worth it. We already know about Trump's palaces (hotels), but I guarantee that we'll learn about all of the secret rooms and tunnels, too.

Trump and the Republican party may be able to suppress the vote enough to win again in 2020. On the bright side, it will finally be socially acceptable to carry a torches or pitchforks in the city.

We vote him out on November 3 or take to the streets on November 4.

6 Definitely Doggerel

Trump Oxymorons

Trump & Honesty
Trump & Constitution
Trump & America
Trump & Truth
Trump & Life

There once was a dude from Brooklyn
Who spent his time as a crook, Lynn
He'd steal and he'd rob
So they gave him the job
Of running the country he'd raped - sin!

There once was a man of the hard sell
Who was insane but faked being well
Lying and boasting
To avoid roasting
45 still ended up in hell

Trump fans are red
Patriots are blue
If I voted for Trump
I'd be embarrassed, too

If I see one more Russian on Facebook
Trying to get me to vote red
I'm gonna wish Trump was gone
And that Joe McCarthy was here instead

Здравствуйте Putin.
Зравствуйте Trump.
Прощай America.

Rah Rah Rasputin
Rah Rah Clump
Russia's got Vladimir Putin
America's got Donald Trump
If I were a betting man
I wouldn't bet on the chump

Big hips, no brain
Let's make Trump
A loser again!

I'd tell Trump to eat shit
If I wasn't worried that
He was into it

If Trump's got Zuckerberg
And a lock on Twitter
Take it to the bank, 2020,
America's going down the shitter

Roses are Red
Russia is, too
Go fuck yourself
If you're not voting blue

One and one is two
Two and two is four
Donald is a prick
And Melania is a ho

I know that my rhymes are crap
And not much more than doggerel
Better that, I say, old chap
Than being a Trump supporterel!

It's only four years of dread
Yet it seems a lifetime ago
When yellow hair atop an orange head
Emerged from Mar-a-Lago

Linus and the Great Pumpkin, now sadly ruined forever by the image of Trump's fat head and orange hair.

The Devil always seems fit
And can play the fiddle in all directions,
But according to Charlie Daniels,
Trump can't play the radio without
Instructions.

There once was a man in a golden room,
Whose dick was so short it was a 'shroom.
He said with a frown,
As he pulled his pants down,
"Melania's gonna leave me for a broom."

There once was a man in the White House
Roared like a lion, but was hung like a mouse.
He didn't pay rent,
And everything he spent,
Came from Putin, in rubles, the louse.

"As the American president
And U.S. main White House resident
I know I don't belong
'Cause my crimes are so strong
And the facts against me are self-evident."

His 2016 "win" was quite shocking
Due to EC* cock blocking
But he cried and he whined
When on hamberders he dined
And FBI warrants for treason came stalking
(*Electoral College)

"It's amazing how I can get away with rape
From trouble like a superhero with no cape
I am a stalker
Who needs a walker
But Bill Barr will help me escape."

There once was an asshole from Queens,
Who got free press quite obscene.
He said with a smirk,
"I know I'm a jerk,
But I've got senators by their spleens."

There once was a man named Donald,
Who resembled Ronald McDonald.
He had the ugly hair,
And total lack of flair,
Like a Trump apartment remodeled.

Donald Trump leading our nation
Is like being caught in tubal ligation.

I can't get untied
Or accept their side,
But we'll solve it by the next election.

"As a fake American president
And yellow-bellied White House resident
My crimes are so strong
And I don't belong:
The facts against me are self-evident."

There once was a loser from Queens,
Whose dick was much too short to be seen.
He cried like a bitch
To his friend #MoscowMitch:
"Nancy Pelosi is making me scream!"

Poetry is sublime
But in the era of Trump
Who's got the time?

It's All Obama's Fault

Why didn't Obama stop Eve from eating the apple?

Where was Obama when Noah needed him?

Why didn't Obama stop James Wilkes Booth?

Where was Obama during the Spanish Inquisition?
Answer me that?!

Obama also screwed the pooch by not keeping Lee
Harvey Oswald out of the U.S. when he came back
from *Russia*.

7 Religion Gone Wrong

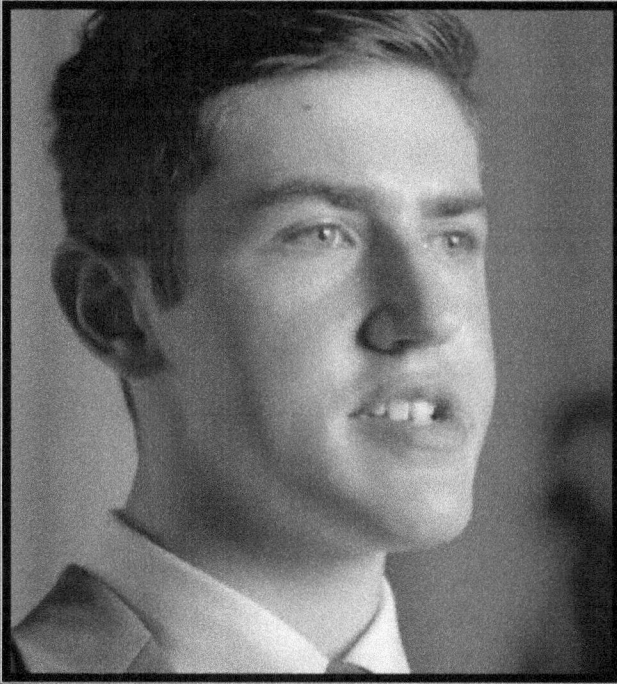

I'M PISSED OFF
MY PARENTS WON'T PAY FOR BRACES

Fake morality is the new morality.

God tells me that Mike Pence is a homosexual.

Evangelicals believe that Trump is leading them to Heaven. Let 'em have it. Think of the party we'll have in Hell!

"I knew your Mom very well. She opitimized being a good Christian. By the way, when Trump was asked if he ever prayed to God for forgiveness, he responded that he might, if he ever were to commit a sin... Just in case he were to make it there - if spectators are permitted on Judgment Day - pack a lunch!" - Art Troutman

"During the last Administration the VA was removing Bibles & even banning Christmas carols to be politically correct, but under President @realDonaldTrump, VA hospitals will NOT be religion-free zones. Message to the New Hampshire VA: the Bible STAYS!" - Trump retweets Pence. "You mean your ambiguously gay sidekick?" - Me

It seems odd that evangelicals defend "religion," but not the teachings of Jesus.

Evangelicals apparently hate profanity more than they hate treason.

Remember when your parents told you that lying was a sin? Apparently, they never read the Trump Bible.

If the god that they believe in actually exists, Trump supporters will soon find out that they have misinterpreted the Bible... very badly.

I often wondered what it might take to create a fake religion, but then Franklin Graham taught me to simply tweak an old one 180 degrees.

Famous Bible Passages: Two Corinthians Walk into a Bar. Trump 1.0.

Can we finally separate America into two countries - the blue states with the innovation and money and the red states with the religion and racism, and make people choose one or the other, and act accordingly?

Someone on Facebook argued that Mike Pompeo's evangelical beliefs are a big factor in his actions as Secretary of State and obfuscation in service of Trump. I don't see religion as guiding Pompeo one tiny bit. It's hypocritical cover for Machiavellian dirty tricks, at best.

I was brought up in the Presbyterian church, I never felt judged. My neighbors didn't hate. In fact, they helped people of every other religion, creed, color, political leaning and sexual orientation.

I met incredibly wonderful people at that church. I'm *proud* to have been a part of that. Fortunately, it was fairly easy: no one that I ever met in church ever came close to resembling Donald Trump. Thank God!

Just the weight of prayers for Trump's demise must add *some* sort of weight on Trump's shoulders. Right? Right? (Rhetorical question.)

Armageddon tired of Trump.

We all have evil and good inside of us. Every one of us can be closer to a Gandhi than a Hitler. Make good choices.

American evangelicals are Pharisees with political power.

How did the Evangelical Right gain so much influence? Anti-abortion plus racism is catnip to low-information voters.

If Mike Pompeo actually "walked with Christ," Jesus would have slapped him silly for working for Donald Trump.

I'm in danger of allowing fake Evangelical "Christians" to make me a bad Christian.

Republicans win elections by rigging voting machines, gerrymandering and voter suppression. Their biggest trick, however, was convincing evangelicals that Republicans don't practice abortion when it's in their own self interest.

The only people who are "pro abortion" are women and men who know that having a baby will ruin their lives. Why not promote sex education, condoms and birth control, and end 99 percent of this nightmare? This issue has given us a country where the American Taliban (evangelicals) and godless Russians have accidentally(?) teamed up to share control of a Russian-selected Manchurian candidate whose crimes are legion against everything that's supposedly sacred.

It seems odd to me how many anti-vaxxers, pro-life and anti-medication-for-depression people exist... and how few of them are medical doctors.

Going high where they go low may get us into Heaven, but it is helping to make America a living Hell.

Sexual desire is wired into humans. Instead of demonizing it and trying to bury it as America does, thus enabling Jeffrey Epsteins and Harvey Weinsteins, why not put everything out in the open, educate young boys and girls about the threats, and be proactive? The lives saved might be those of your own children.

Anti-abortionists gave us Trump.

Legislation in Ohio could require teachers to accept scientifically inaccurate, faith-based answers to homework assignments. Welcome to the new Dark Ages.

HypoChristians will be the death of us all.

The God that Republican senators and evangelical Christians are referring to is Mammon.

When a Trump supporter says, "I'll pray for you," it means _____.

When you think of Jesus, which Republican politicians come to mind?

You care about your stock portfolio. You're afraid of people of color and any religion besides your own. We see you. It's not flattering.

Angry? Check. Irreligious? Check. Against Trump? Check. Anti-American? Hell no!

If there's a nuclear war because of Trump's insanity, evangelicals finally got their wish.

Revengelicals ™ want Rapture, but what they'll give all of us is Armageddon.

Trump's going to screw up so badly soon that there will be no press conference or announcement walking it back. It will be beyond disastrous. And anyone thinking that Armageddon is going to get them into Heaven is going to be greatly surprised.

I wonder what pro-life adherents would do if they had a chance to go back in time and abort Hitler and Stalin. If all lives matter, what about the millions killed because of such monsters? Didn't they count?

All of these millionaire "Christians" seem to have forgotten the camel and the eye of the needle story.

Whenever I see a preacher holding a bible up in the air over Donald Trump's head, I envision that the Bible is a brick and the "preacher" was going to put Trump out of our misery. Then I wonder to myself, is that wrong?

What will St. Peter say to Donald Trump if he winds up at the Pearly Gates? (A purely rhetorical question.)

I don't believe that God will punish the wicked. Why not? Dictators who lived out their lives peacefully include Josef Stalin, Mao Zedong, Francois "Papa Doc" Duvalier, Kim Il-sung and Augusto Pinochet. That's why.

I was brought up Presbyterian. Compared to that, today's evangelicalism is Scientology squared.

God, if you're up there, I'm not happy about my behavior in the age of Trump. I'm not as good at aiming high as the Obamas. If I *am* forgiven, however, I will have some very hard and pointed questions for you when I finally get to see you.

You hate abortion? Show your support by proving your financial to donations poor black women with fetuses in ghettos.

God told me that Pat Robertson uses Trump's hand-me-down Depends.

If Roe v. Wade is overturned, women will die getting abortions in alleys... as will their fetuses. When millions of those fetuses die, who's pro life?

"I'm a Christian." - Donald Trump. "Being a Christian no longer has meaning." - Me

With apologies to
Pastor Martin Niemoeller

I'm not Mexican, but Trump came for Mexicans first.

I'm not Muslim, but Trump came for Muslims next.

I'm not black, but Trump's policies target blacks unfairly.

I'm not Jewish, but Trump defended Nazis in Charlottesville.

I'm not gay, but Trump is taking away my gay friends' rights.

I'm not in the military, but Trump is deporting men and women who fought for America.

I'm not handicapped, but Trump is taking away rights from the handicapped.

I'm not homeless, but Trump has "a plan" for homeless people.

When will you wake up and realize that when Trump has cleared America of all the above that he won't come for white Democrats?

And then Republicans who are not loyal enough?

And when all of those people are gone, you know what you'll have? Nazi Germany 2.0.

8 Cracked Questions

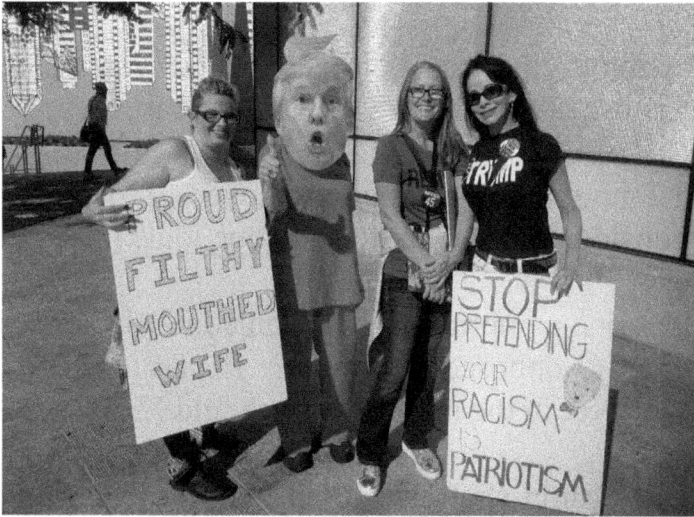

How is having Trump Derangement Syndrome worse than being unaware or purposely blind of Trump's atrocities?

Fame and oodles of money apparently leads to pedophilia. Who knew?

How can you go any lower than an oligarchy run by a fascist?

Who is Donald Trump? The Grinch, without the awakening? An evil villain who morphed into Trump after a thermonuclear war? A character in a dystopian novel who escaped from its pages to wreak havoc on America?

Power corrupts, and absolute power corrupts absolutely. Money is power. Bill Cosby. Harvey Weinstein. Jeffrey Epstein. Alex Acosta. Donald Trump. Alan Dershowitz.

Bill Barr. Who has time to wait for Satan to take them all back?

If your parents gave you a girl's name, but you were a boy, would Lindsey Graham take your health care away?

Donald Trump administration employees, remember when it was considered bad form to sell your soul?

How does one compromise with someone whose ideals are diametrically opposed to mine? If Trumpsters aren't willing to meet in the middle, why should I?

If Donald Trump shot and killed me on 5th Avenue, and you were a Republican, would you care?

What father that you ever knew placed his hands on his daughter's hips? Besides Trump?

Why do we always have to accommodate the fear and hatred of racists? Can't we put more emphasis on rationality?

Where are all the American patriots standing up against President Stephen Miller?

We need to give in to the Waltons and Kochs. After all, their money makes them a billion times better than us, right?

When Trump closes our borders to emigration, will you finally wake up?

What do we have, if we don't have hope?

Donald Trump wanted to turn America into pre-revolutionary France. Can't you just see Jeff Sessions or Bill Barr throwing a starving man into jail for 20 years for stealing a loaf of bread?

Here's a simple question to every person in the U.S. armed forces: "Did you take an oath to the Constitution, or to the latest president?" Your answers will be on your permanent record.

As Trump, er, Hitler, foretold, when steady jobs and incomes fall, fill the populace with economic fear, find a scapegoat, then direct the populace to attack that scapegoat to save the "status" that you've bestowed upon them. What have I missed?

Want a public-school education in America? Got body armor?

Obama showed his birth certificate, so when will Donald Trump show his taxes?

How can Trump sue Stormy Daniels for breaking their non-disclosure agreement if what she says never happened?

If I was the president and I truly loved America, I would follow policies that would be good for America and the world. Why won't Trump?

What is the religious reason to be "good," considering America's current "leadership?"

Donald Trump is making demands. Where in the Constitution does it say that he's the emperor?

I wonder what our national blood pressure is now, compared to pre-Trump?

What's the difference between liberals and conservatives? Conservatives don't know that "Democraps" and "libtards" have guns, too.

Where are America's adults?

Which Obama policy made Republicans so hate the son of a married Christian white American woman who never had an abortion?

Was praying for bombshells in Bob Mueller's potential testimony... Democrats in the House to show backbone... or Republicans in the Senate to show integrity... intelligent patriotism or just a stupid pipe dream?

The three least understood words in the U.S. Constitution? "Well-Regulated Militia."

If ISIS was committing more than one mass shooting per day in America, how long would our current politicians remain in office?

Some people say, "Eat the rich." Most wealthy people are old and gamey. Eat the kids of the rich?

Seeing people defend Donald Trump online, I wonder where Russians learned such good English. Trump University?

Remember the good old days, when our grandfathers had to fight fascists thousands of miles away in Europe?

Sean Spicer still gets hired. How is that possible?

Is the worst reality TV show in history finally coming to a close?

Donald Trump said that Nancy Pelosi's bringing of impeachment charges ruined his day. Can we all chip in and send him a waaaaambulance?

Who will launder Russia's money if our Dear Trumper goes to the federal penitentiary?!

Trump: Toddler? Tyrant? Traitor?

Trump supporters... Where *do* you buy your Whataboutism?

Q. How do you lose money operating a casino? A. "What is, laundering money for the Russians?"

If there was a Deep State, don't you think that we'd have seen Trump's taxes a helluva lot sooner?

If Donald Trump is going to sue people, shouldn't he take them to Small Hands Court?

When fascists control each of America's defenses against fascism, is it surprising that America became a fascist state?

What will Bill Barr do for Rudy Giuliani, now that Rudy is in danger of being arrested? Rub his back in the penitentiary?

When Trump takes his tax case to the highest court, as you know he will, how many members of the Supreme Court will allow themselves to go down in history as traitors to the rule of law?

Robert Mueller wasted our time and killed our hopes. Can't indict a sitting president? Where in the criminal code is that bullshit?

Nancy Pelosi's got balls. Trump's got... er... malls?

Why can't Jim Jordan wear suitcoats? Do they represent honesty to him?

Mike Pence wants to revoke LGBTQ protections. Why would he want to take away rights from himself?

What's the matter with Kentucky?

What would happen if you or I ignored a subpoena?

If conservative right-wing supporters care so much about abortion, where are all of the Trump and Osteen orphanages?

Devin Nunes' bloviating tells me that he hates the media. Can you imagine where we'd be without investigative journalism?

What has Putin wanted that Trump hasn't given him for free? I mean, besides Ivanka?

How much you wanna bet that Trump pisses on the toilet seat?

If laws regarding the presidency no longer matter, what laws do?

I'm raring to go on November 3, 2020. But I'm talking about *now*. Where are America's heroes in the S*enate*?

When do the 65 million Americans who voted against Trump get our say?

People insult me because of my anger over Trump's dismantling of America. Here's my question: Why aren't *you* angry?

Won't *one* Republican senator stand up against Putin? WTF?

Amy Coney Barrett: Stepford Justice.

"Fake Melania" cracks me up. The *real* Melania is all fake!

Facebook obviously knows everything about us. So why do they allow us to see what people who are diametrically opposed to us say... unless they're making money off of our division?

Trump is using and abusing the military for his own purposes. When will the military wake up?

Why is professionalism and perfection required of the FBI, but only rank amateurism for the president?

Trump supporters post such bizarre and stupid statements on social media. Don't they understand that in 100 years, people will still be laughing at their dumb asses?

If Kellyanne Conway had her own scent, what would it be called - Skank, Alternative Farts, Or Bowling Green Massacre: The Scent?

When will Russia release Donald Trump's campaign emails?

Can Yosemite Sam sue Trump for stupidity?

Ladies, what's Donald Trump's most attractive feature?

Witch doctor is Trump promoting today?

If you support Trump, then you support children locked up in cages. What happened to your soul?

Trump wants to kill the U.S. Postal Service, which has served America since 1775. Trump has "served" since 2017. Does anyone else see a problem with this besides me?

Trump is concentrated evil. Rebuttals?

When did Nazi symbols come to represent something positive for a certain portion of Americans?

Dr. Anthony Fauci is getting death threats for speaking truth about the Coronavirus. America, what happened to you?

Someone asked if Donald Trump writes his own speeches. I said that he writes nothing except checks to porn stars. Rebuttals?

How can you say you love America if you've never been out of your own state?

If Bill Barr was billed at a bar, would Bill Barr be barred or blackballed for a bad check, or would Bill Barr be pardoned by a pathetic president purely to piss off people the president had potentially peed upon?

Having a Postmaster General purposely delay the mail leading up to a presidential election is like, I dunno, election rigging?

Remember all of Melania Trump's successes with her anti-bullying campaign?

Crazy thought: Trumpian arguments always argue against free stuff and how hard they work. How about a 1-1 comparison to the average worker in a red state to that of an average worker in a blue state? And who pays more in taxes?

Does anyone find it odd that Trump is actively killing off his voting base?

People attack me for my mean and cutting words. It's a personal choice I made long ago. Would you prefer bullets?

The U.S. was simply not prepared for the Coronavirus. Where's the buck supposed to stop?

Trump represents cowardly old white racist fascist wannabe oligarchs like those that Putin controls in Russia. How am I wrong?

Trump supporters are hate-filled morons or oblivious and apathetic. Is there no the middle ground?

What has the Trump administration done for America besides fuck it up?

What desires of Vladimir Putin has Donald Trump not fulfilled?

What good are your vaunted civil liberties when your grandparents die of TrumpVirus, you can't drink the water, oceans are polluted and you can't eat the fish?

What if Trump *is* the virus?

Reasons to Be Ridin' with Biden

Biden has a soul. Trump has a bunker.
Biden doesn't spend hours a day on his hair.
Biden doesn't paint himself orange.
Biden has a wife who's not a porn star.
Biden has lost two daughters and a son. Trump ignores a son.
Biden actually has empathy." - Joe Gunn
Biden's not Trump: winning!

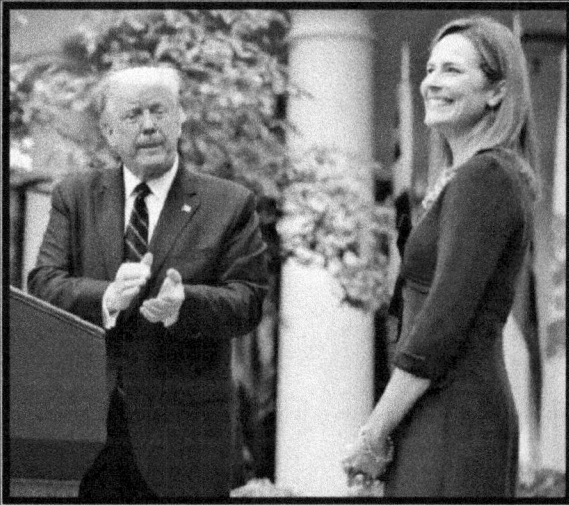

NEVER TRUST A MAN WHO WEARS

MORE MAKEUP THAN A WOMAN

Donald Trump and Mike Pence Go Camping

As a bonding exercise before the 2020 election, administration aides suggested that Donald Trump and Mike Pence go camping.

After a dinner of hamberders and Covfefe, Trump and Pence lay down for the night in the White House Rose Garden and went to sleep.

Some hours later, Trump awoke and nudged his sycophantic sidekick.

"Pence, look up at the sky and tell me what you see."

Pence replied, "I see millions of stars."

"What does that tell you?"

Pence pondered for a minute. Was this some sort of twisted test from Trump?

"Well, astronomically, it tells me that there are millions of galaxies and potentially billions of planets.

"Astrologically, I observe that Saturn is in Leo.

"Horologically, I deduce that the time is approximately a quarter past three.

"Theologically, I can see that God is all powerful and that we are small and insignificant.

"Meteorologically, I suspect that we will have a beautiful day tomorrow.

"What does it tell you, Mr. President?"

Trump was silent for a minute, then spoke: "Pence, you idiot. Someone has stolen our tent!"

(* With apologies to the writer of the original story, rated the funniest joke of the year in 2001.)

The Terrific Tower of Trump!

I
Am
The
Loser
You Know:
Don Trump
The Big Loser
Trump Cheated.
Trump is a dotard.
Trump is flat broke.
Hillary actually won.
Trump projects like mad.
Trump's tweets are all lies.
Trump's Putin's cock holster.
Trump caught a Chinese hoax.
Trump inherited $400 million!
Trump blew every damn dollar!!
Trump hires only the best losers!!!
Trump lies like the thing on his head.
Trump bing bong bong bing bing bing!
Trump is America's king of bankruptcy!
Trump got schlonged by Vladimir Putin!
Trump defeats low energy with Adderall.
Trump golf's greatest cheater in the world!
Trump is America's first treasonous president.
Trump of Wharton graduated with no transcripts.

ME

WHEN TRUMP IS FINALLY GONE!

This was the original back cover design.
Kinda depressing, right?

THIS IS THE BACK COVER.
COVER AS IN COVERUP.
COVERUP AS IN THE DEEP STATE.
WHICH DOESN'T EXIST,
BUT TRUMP NEEDS TO PRETEND IT DOES,
SO HE CAN BLAME EVERYONE ELSE
FOR HIS OWN FAILURES.
HASN'T HE ALREADY HIRED
AND FIRED EVERYONE
WHO HASN'T ALREADY QUIT?
ONE THING I GUARANTEE WE'LL GET
IF TRUMP GETS A SECOND TERM:
THE AMERICAN CARNAGE HE'S
PROMISED US SINCE
HIS INAUGURATION DAY.

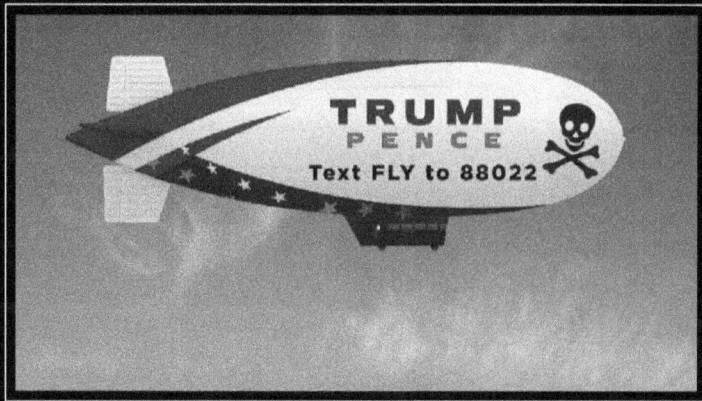

BAD YEAR BLIMP

Metaphor for 2020:

https://tinyurl.com/yx9n849j

Dana Hall Kennon was a lovely woman who helped me to keep going when I was down. As she was slowly dying of cancer, she asked if she could have a quote in my next book. Her quote is in the photograph below.

Dana, you are greatly missed, and many of us fight on in your name. Rest in peace, lovely lady.

"Be my voice, merge it with yours so that I still can be heard and have a say against the evil fighting us."

Dana Hall Kennon

You will not be forgotten

What keeps me alive in the time of Trump is envisioning the party we'll have when he's finally gone.

Books By This Author

Wheelers, Dealers, Pucks & Bucks: A Rocking History of Roller Hockey International
The story of a professional roller hockey league that rose with the popularization of the inline skate, and faded like a fad.

MURPH: The Sports Entrepreneur Man and His Leagues
(Editor)
The autobiography of Dennis Arthur Murphy, the most prolific sports league founder and entrepreneur you've never heard of.

Graham Cracks 1: Turning Beer Into Literature One Joke at a Time
First in a series of joke books.

Graham Cracks 2: Only Jokes Can Save Us Now
Second in a series of joke books.

Graham Cracks 3: Shirley, I Jest!
Third in a series of joke books.

Trumpsters & Traitors: Alternative Facts are Lies and Most Jokes Are True
Political satire and jokes in the age of Trump.

Trumpsters & Traitor 2: Trump or America, Your Choice
More political satire and jokes in the age of Trump.